LAUTRÉAMONT

by Wallace Fowlie

This study is an effort to consider afresh a literary work of the nineteenth century whose influence continues to grow in the twentieth century. During the one hundred years of its existence in print, *Les Chants de Maldoror* has puzzled readers and inspired several contradictory interpretations.

In proposing primarily a psychoanalytical analysis of the work, Wallace Fowlie does not neglect the literary sources and especially the role Lautréamont has played in the development of Surrealism.

The conclusion of this introductory study is an attempt to define Lautréamont's relationship with various aspects of the so-called movement of Decadence at the end of the nineteenth century.

TWAYNE'S WORLD AUTHORS SERIES

A Survey of the World's Literature

Sylvia E. Bowman, Indiana University

GENERAL EDITOR

FRANCE

Maxwell A. Smith, Guerry Professor of French, Emeritus
The University of Chattanooga
Former Visiting Professor in Modern Languages
The Florida State University

EDITOR

Lautréamont

(TWAS 284)

TWAYNE'S WORLD AUTHORS SERIES (TWAS)

The purpose of TWAS is to survey the major writers--
novelists, dramatists, historians, poets, philosophers, and
critics—of the nations of the world. Among the national
literatures covered are those of Australia, Canada, China,
Eastern Europe, France, Germany, Greece, India, Italy,
Japan, Latin America, the Netherlands, New Zealand,
Poland, Russia, Scandinavia, Spain, and the African
nations, as well as Hebrew, Yiddish, and Latin Classical
literature. This survey is complemented by Twayne's United
States Authors Series and English Authors Series.

The intent of each volume in these series is to present
a critical-analytical study of the works of the writer;
to include biographical and historical material that may
be necessary for understanding, appreciation, and critical
appraisal of the writer; and to present all material in clear,
concise English—but not to vitiate the scholarly content
of the work by doing so.

Lautréamont

By Wallace Fowlie

Duke Universitv

ABOUT THE AUTHOR

Wallace Fowlie has been James B. Duke, profes-
sor of French at Duke University since 1964.
Earlier he taught at Yale University and Benning-
ton College. He looks upon this book on Lau-
tréamont as a continuation of his already pub-
lished studies on *Rimbaud, Mallarmé* and *Age
of Surrealism.* His most recent publication is
French Literature: Its History and Its Meaning
(Prentice-Hall, 1973). Other books by Wallace
Fowlie include *Love in Literature: Studies in
Symbolic Expression; Paul Claudel; A Guide to
Contemporary French Literature; Dionysus in
Paris: A Guide to Contemporary French Theater;
A Reading of Proust; André Gide: His Life and
Art; Jean Cocteau: The History of a Poet's Age;
Climate of Violence: The French Literary Tra-
dition from Baudelaire to the Present; The French
Critic;* and *Stendhal.*

ɴew York

Library of Congress Cataloging in Publication Data

Fowlie, Wallace, 1908–
    Lautréamont.
    (Twayne's world authors series, TWAS 284. France)
    Bibliography: p.
    1. Ducasse, Isidore Lucien, 1846–1870.
PQ2220.D723Z654   841'.8   73–14588
ISBN 0–8057–2511–3

To Olivier Revault d'Allonnes

Contents

Chronology

1846   April 4: Birth of Isidore Ducasse, only child of François Ducasse and Jacquette Davezac, in Montevideo, Uruguay.

1847   November 16: Baptism.
       9 December. Death of Isidore's mother, probably by suicide.

1859   October: Begins his studies as a boarding pupil *(interne)* at the *lycée impérial* of Tarbes (today called *lycée* Théophile Gautier).

1862   August: Leaves the *lycée* of Tarbes.

1863   October: Enrolls in the *lycée de Pau, classe de rhétorique* (1863–1864).

1864– *Classe de philosophie, lycée de Pau.*
1865

1865– Probably lives in Tarbes.
1867

1867   In the fall of the year, comes to Paris where he lives in a hotel at 23, rue Notre-Dame-des-Victoires.

1868   August: Publication of *Le Chant Premier,* printed by Balitout, Questroy et Cie. Unsigned.

1869   January: *Le Chant Premier* is published for the second time in the collection *Les parfums de l'âme.* Summer: *Les Chants de Maldoror* is published by Lacroix, in Brussels. October. Isidore Ducasse is living at 32, rue du Faubourg-Montmartre.

1870   February: Moves to 15, rue Vivienne. July: Moves to 7, Faubourg-Montmartre. September: Paris under siege of the Prussian army. November 24: Ducasse dies in his hotel, 7, Faubourg-Montmartre. He was 24 years old.

CHAPTER 1

Introduction

EVERYTHING about Lautréamont is unusual. He is unique in the history of French literature in the strange forcefulness emanating from his writing. Although his influence during the latter part of the nineteenth century was negligible, his example and *Les Chants de Maldoror* helped to open up in the twentieth century a new beginning in literature and art. The Surrealists placed him very high among the forerunners and practitioners of their movement. Breton, Eluard, Soupault, and Tzara in particular extolled his work and defined the prophetic aspects of his legacy. Individual writers continued to assess his importance: Gide, Camus, Cocteau, Aimé Césaire, Bonnefoy, Aragon. The attention paid to Lautréamont by critics in general, and by several of the most incisive and penetrating critics of the twentieth century, has sustained interest in *Maldoror* and encouraged investigation: Bachelard, Praz, Bataille, Sollers, Béguin, Blanchot, Raymond, Nadeau, Caillois.

His name is usually associated with Arthur Rimbaud, and with good reason, as the kind of writer who established new relationships between things, and alliances between the old established logic with the logic of a man's instinct. This power of joining in a literary work processes of thought accessible to everyone, with a personal secretive method, is the mark of a major writer. Lautréamont reveals a more savage ferociousness than Rimbaud, a more brutal eroticism, but both of them seem to have had a basically ingenuous nature expressing very primitive needs.

In the history of French literature, Rimbaud and Lautréamont, writing about 1870, came at a moment when Romanticism had worn itself out and when the new writers, coming soon after the death of Baudelaire in 1867, began asking such leading questions as: What is the essence of art? What is the literary phenomenon? Does a literary success correspond to the intentions of a writer? These questions, which form the major preoccupations of critics today, are in Lautréamont, but they went unheeded for some time.

Other matters held the attention of the first critics and the first serious readers.

I *The Secretiveness of His Life*

The absence of biographical information concerning Isidore Ducasse was a curious phenomenon in the annals of modern literature. Even those critics who repudiate a biographical approach to a literary figure seem troubled by this lack in Lautréamont's case. This very absence threw into greater relief than ever the extraordinary personality of Rimbaud and the literal story of his life. And then, the blatant extravagances in *Les Chants* attracted too easily the attention of critics: all the bombastic traits and the buffoonery, the macabre and the lycanthropy, the many reminiscences of the Gothic tale and the *feuilleton*.

Gradually attention has been focused on more significant matters: on the personal and secretive human drama which the text is beginning to reveal; on those moments, or episodes, of intense beauty in the text which reveal both the exacerbated sensibility of Lautréamont and the power of his imagination; on the schizophrenic nature of this youthful writer. The early theory of Lautréamont's madness has now been discarded. The deliberate organized structure of the work would invalidate any such theory. But there is a dichotomy, a drama in itself, between the primitive impulsiveness of Isidore Ducasse and the controlled aloofness of le comte de Lautréamont. The personality and the actions of Maldoror are perhaps best explained as being the fusion of Ducasse and Lautréamont, of the young man living realistically and imaginatively his human experience, and the same young man who recasts this same experience into a work of art. It is the same man who hurls himself onto objects and beings in the world and makes of them prey to his physical and sexual hunger, and the haughty figure who exploits these two kinds of hunger by calling up from his subconscious the obscure forces that reside there.

Sincerity, or what is usually called sincerity in one man's relationship with other human beings, has nothing to do with art. The artist, to create his art, has to be someone different from what he is in his ordinary life. *Les Chants de Maldoror* is a very histrionic example of this duality of man the artist. Society holds in check most of man's inclinations to sarcasm and revolt and vituperation. But the artist, under his seeming obedience to the rules of normal behavior and the exigencies of his daily life, nurtures a spirit of revolt and gives expression to it in his work. He often prefigures and justifies the literal revolutions that come after him in history. The tepid mediocre historical period in which Lautréamont and Rimbaud lived was followed by a series of wars lasting until today which have made the actions and the behavior of Maldoror familiar to us. Romanticism, of which Lautréamont is a representative, is that form of literature the most apt to translate the dramas, the fantasies, the insults of the subconscious. His book is, in a way, the triumph of the subconscious. From beginning to end, he remains the type of man whom ordinary conscious life is unable to satisfy. The tone of discontent is sustained and renewed throughout the writing. It remains as strident as the music of Berlioz and as colorful as the paintings of Delacroix.

II   *The Possibility of Paranoia*

This restitution of his inner subconscious life, which his book represented, was both recompense for the drab existence Ducasse seems to have led, and a revenge. The modest Parisian hotel room where he lived and wrote was the literal habitation of the apocryphal comte de Lautréamont. The second personality avenged the first by the exaltation of human cruelty in episode after episode of *Les Chants de Maldoror*. The silence and the anonymity of Isidore Ducasse were avenged in the motivated rebellion of Lautréamont.

Definitions of paranoia, perversity and madness have undergone many changes in recent times. Today the art of Lautréamont no longer seems unaccountably strange. Before him and after him the cases are now numerous of those writers who were broken by the stresses of society, who joined the ranks of the alienated, but whose art is owing at least in part to the conflict between the emergence of a personality and the forces bent upon making it conform.

These are the neurotic, *les grands nerveux* as Proust calls them in a passage of *Le côté de Guermantes* when Dr. du Boulbon says to Marcel's grandmother, «*Vous êtes le sel de la terre.*» The neurotics are those who created masterpieces and founded religions. Rousseau, Poe, Baudelaire, Hölderlin, Nietzsche, Dostoevski, Wilde are a few of the names so often rehearsed in this regard. But why not Homer the blind wanderer, and Dante the wanderer in exile? Why not Rimbaud who called his life on this earth a season in hell? Why not Lautréamont who was more scornful of society than Byron had been, and who was probably more fully conscious of this conflict than his contemporary, Arthur Rimbaud? Of all of these writers, Lautréamont was the most negative, the most pessimistic concerning all forms of sociability, all forms of human constraint.

We are able to speak in a so-called intelligible manner only because we accept verbal conventions, only because we have learned forms of compromise and abdication. Lautréamont, when he refers to easily understood writers, Chateaubriand and Hugo, for example, derides them: Chateaubriand *le Mohican mélancolique,* and Hugo *le funèbre échalas-vert* (vineprop). René's *mal du siècle* in the American forest, and Hugo's facile antitheses, seem almost commonplaces by comparison with the new reign instituted by *Les Chants de Maldoror,* the reign of spleen and neurosis, the reign of disproportionate things, the reign of the man who sees in the world only himself and God, and who is irked by the presence of God. Maldoror is insulted by his fate. He can accept it only if he spends his time seeking the clue to its mystery. He therefore tests and explores all forms of anomalies in his search.

Most books are the continuation of the recognizable daily ways in which men live and love and suffer. In so-called popular books, as in popular films, the rhythm of daily events and happenings is accelerated. The swift tempo with which the action unfolds in *Fantômas,* and *Les trois mousquetaires,* in westerns and the James Bond films, in thrillers, gives to these works an almost supernatural intensity. By speeding up action, it is made to appear magical. Is life, after all, at least in its dire moments, a trap of the gods?

These characteristics of popular art are in *Les Chants de Maldoror.* Their sensationalism approaches the supernatural. In the youthfulness of his ambition, Lautréamont certainly sought devices, processes of thought and sensations that would appear new and startling. Today we are more held by what lies behind the exterior expression of sarcasm and the formal pattern that intended to shock. The work itself today seems to us less mysterious than what it opens onto. And that, indeed, is something infinitely mysterious, something comparable to the dawn on the sea or a man's subconscious.

In the last analysis, a book is judged by the effect it has on its readers, by the influence it creates, by the kind of stimulation it engenders. The majority of writers who have recorded their reaction to Lautréamont are on the whole noncommittal and pass over the problem with such a statement as that of Marcel Arland's: *un livre des plus curieux*. Others have acknowledged an unwillingness or an inability to give a careful reading. Valéry explained why he read only very little of Lautréamont by saying that when he received the book, he received at the same time the small volume of *Les Illuminations*. The reading of Rimbaud was so overpowering an experience for him that Lautréamont lost out.

III   *The Surrealist Cult*

A deep sympathy for Lautréamont, which was true of many Surrealists, made them feel it was useless to write about him, useless to try to explain his power and his significance. Lautréamont became a secret cult which was beyond explanation. Eluard, for example, based his silence on the fact that France despises poetry. *A quoi bon parler de Lautréamont? La France a horreur de la vraie poésie.* Henri Michaux claimed it is useless to analyze and explain the position of Lautréamont. It lies beyond the domain of criticism which must content itself with explaining the straightforward professional man of letters: Cicero, La Bruyère, Bazin. Cocteau summarized the problem in a typically aphoristic manner by saying that we don't explain what we live in or frequent, that for some time we have been inhabiting the "Isidore-Arthur Establishment," to which he adds three other names including his own: *Nous habitons la Maison Isidore-Arthur et Cie, Max, Radiguet et Cocteau.*

Les Chants de Maldoror and *Poésies* are works of a psychological Romanticism. They are works of deep feeling that concern revolt or negation. They negate the positive forces of life as lyrically, as ecstatically as the *Inferno* does. They are the story of an unhappy adolescent who writes when he is intoxicated with negation.

Dante had to go through the darkness of hell before he could come before the vision of the stars. Lautréamont remains within his *Inferno*. He is unable to move beyond his adolescent preferences for evil and darkness, for melancholy and death. The metamorphoses of Maldoror recall similar phenomena of the Gothic tale, but they are also phenomena inherent in puberty and later adolescence when a boy's imagination forces him into roles of sexual conquest.

What Racine owed to Euripides in his composition of *Phèdre* is fairly easy to ascertain. The sources of Maldoror are of a different nature. Throughout the work, Dante and Sade come to mind frequently. They must have been readings that helped to form the mind of Isidore Ducasse. Figures, obsessions, and atmosphere from the *Inferno* and the writings of the Marquis de Sade must have encouraged and confirmed the natural bent of the young man's imagination, in changing him from Ducasse to Lautréamont. His very youthfulness permitted him to carry out the pact between the life of his imagination and his ambition to be a writer.

The richness of imagery in Lautréamont is equaled only by the richness of imagery in Rimbaud. These two adolescent works of the few years that preceded and followed 1870 mark a turning point in French literature, which was not fully realized until the advent of Surrealism in the twentieth century. Morbidity, cruelty, perverseness are normal traits in the very young. When they return later in the temperament of a mature man, they are not always recognized as traits of the child. In the literary tradition, the Surrealists, largely because of their study of Sade and Lautréamont, celebrated man's cruelty as a continuing force of childhood and as a necessary preparation for man's revolt against society.

IV *The Horror of Convention*

The prisons of childhood, school, family, church, encourage the practice of dreaming and the planned ravishment of the world. Children live imaginatively the sexual and social accomplishments of adulthood. Adulthood is often a bitter resentment against the disparity between the dreams of the child and the meager accomplishments of the grown man. The Roman emperors who perpetrated acts of cruelty and bloodshed were often adolescents. The long prison terms of Sade encouraged his sexual obsessions and gave him the time to write out his dreams.

Dominating and incorporating all these secondary themes in Lautréamont, the major theme of the writings might be named the adolescent's horror for conventional life, for what Baudelaire and Flaubert called the *esprit bourgeois.* This sense of horror lies behind the firm vigorous sentences, the vehemence and the humor, the balanced cadences, the unexpected metaphors, the verbal plethora, all the exasperated romanticism of literary expression. Today we would like to know from what unknown psychic sources these *chants* rose up. No fully satisfactory explanation can be reached. But such literary-psychological search continues and will continue. Already we can probably see farther into these personal and cosmic conflicts than Lautréamont himself saw. In a very real sense, each human being is inviolable. The private dramas of a man do not belong to us. With the author of *Les Chants de Maldoror* we tend to ask—did he ever exist in the human community? But then we realize that the same question can be raised about every man. There is no portrait of Lautréamont, no death mask, no reproduction comparable to Pascal's or Baudelaire's tragic face. Lautréamont's inviolability is better preserved than that of most writers.

Biographical research of the scholars has, on the whole, turned out to be futile. In their approach to *Les Chants* and *Poésies,* most critics tend to simplify their explanations by applying one word, such as "mad," "surreal," "absurd." Or they tend to define the moving force in the work as evil, and the sexual activity they discover as sadistic. The title *Poésies* is harder to qualify, and, again, an overfacile meaning is often given to the term when it is called the result of the dichotomy between common sense and imagination.

It has been customary to apply such a word as "rational" to literature of the seventeenth and eighteenth centuries, and "irrational" to at least some of the literature of the nineteenth century, and especially to such a work as *Maldoror.* But the term "rational" is seen today to be harder to define accurately than ever before in history. And those human activities to which the word "rational" is traditionally applied are seen today to be little more than states of camouflage. The real activities of a man transpire behind the screen of his so-called rational behavior. Literature, whether it is the sonnets of Shakespeare, *La Chartreuse de Parme* of Stendhal, or *Les Chants de Maldoror,* is the closest revelation we have of man's inner life where he reenacts ancient myths or dreams not consonant with his daily external life. From childhood on, we learn to obscure desires and to rechannel instincts. Our so-called age of reason is the age when we learn that our real life cannot be lived in society, that precisely an art of camouflage has to be devised so that we may exist on two levels: one in the community of men, and one in the loneliness of the spirit which is also the freedom of the spirit.

Every writer whose work has continued to be meaningful is a scapegoat taking unto himself the guilt of humanity, representing humanity in its truest state, revealing what a man under the conditions of his ordinary life is disinclined or unable to reveal. The art of literature, in its highest form, is the catharsis of the irrational. The close study of literature inevitably leads us to a renewed belief in the value and the power of the irrational in man. Outside of literature, the study of man, when restricted to his behavior, in society, in his family, in his church, in his vocation, will provide only a partial and often misleading picture of him. Most men are patient hypocrites. The writer too is often that in his social life. But in his writing he can be, as Lautréamont was, a volcanic manifestation, an explosive force resulting from the repressions of hypocrisy and patience.

As the Revolution of 1789 exploded after three centuries of monarchy and seeming political stability imposed on the French, as the Gothic tale appeared in France after two centuries of so-called Classicism in literature and art, so *Maldoror* came out of a sensibility that had been repressed in all the usual patterns of modern life and probably in some unusual patterns that biographers will never discover. That mental life of an adolescent, usually relegated to the limbo of the subconscious, was given its literary expressions in *Les Chants.* The aggressiveness of Lautréamont had doubtless been totally suppressed in the real life of Isidore Ducasse. It is cast into an extreme form of aggressiveness: animal-like and monstrous.

V *Metamorphosis*

The recurrent theme of transformations probably has its source in the adolescent dream of becoming someone else, of taking on the dreamed-of characteristics of powerful or attractive beings who would compensate for all ineffectual traits of the real self. Maldoror is metamorphosed into an eagle, a crab, a vulture, a cricket, an octopus, a shark. But the magical beauty of Maldoror himself and his supernatural powers of seduction and destruction represent the supreme metamorphosis in the work.

Such a complete metamorphosis permits the use of invective and blasphemy; indeed it requires such expression because the book is the revenge over the silence and the anonymity of a human life. "Revenge" is almost too mild a word to designate the fury and the passion of some of the pages of *Maldoror*. The myth of the "exterminating angel" would seem to be the scenario behind many of the actual episodes. At frequent intervals in the text, Lautréamont sets out to comment on the work, to explain what he is writing. Such beginnings are usually interrupted by flashes of self-mockery and self-judgment. Each time Lautréamont begins to explain the literary effort he is making, he ends by questioning the value of literature, or more precisely the limitations of literature. Since the world has betrayed him, isn't it possible that literature too will betray him? The writer, and especially the young writer, needs to be the accuser, and he assumes this role automatically when he celebrates the irrational more than the rational, and the chances of darkness more than the order of light.

But Lautréamont constantly argues that it is rational to celebrate the irrational. The faultless syntax of his writing and the carefully written sentences joined in logical sequence accentuate the reasonableness of the disorder in all six cantos. He constructs a labyrinth (Nietzsche would call this the Apollonian aspect of the work) in order to lead us into the heart of the most troublesome dilemmas, into the scenes of Dionysian frenzy and madness from which there seems to be no escape. Rimbaud spoke of the sacredness of his mind's disorder, and Lautréamont constructed scene after scene demonstrating the activity of that disorder. Myths having the anonymity that he first wished to give to his *Chants* are those stories that provide means of communication between the conscious and subconscious states of a man. *Les Chants* draws upon the myths or stories that resemble mythic patterns for a similar purpose of providing a passageway back and forth between the rational and irrational, the emotional and intellectual, the clear consciousness of the mind and the dark subconscious of the spirit.

CHAPTER 2

Biographical Facts and Surmises

I Montevideo

DESPITE the scanty biographical information concerning Isidore Ducasse, two books about his life have recently been published (Peyrouzet, *Vie de Lautréamont,* 1970, and Caradec, *Isidore Ducasse, comte de Lautréamont,* 1970) which help to correct misinterpretations and legends that have been repeated countless times in articles and prefaces, and that provide background material on members of his family, acquaintances, and places where he lived.

Both parents, Francois Ducasse and Jacquette Davezac, came from the region of the Pyrenees. His father was first a schoolteacher in Sarniguet, a small town near Tarbes. At the age of thirty, probably in 1840, Francois Ducasse went to South America where he settled in Montevideo, Uruguay. He worked at the French consulate, holding the modest position of *commis chancelier.* In the early forties, one-third of the population of Montevideo was European. The French, primarily Basques, had settled there in large numbers where they were mainly small craftsmen or businessmen.

Isidore-Lucien, the only child of the Ducasses, was born on February 21, 1846, in Montevideo, where Jules Laforgue was born a few years later (1860), and where Jules Supervielle was born still later (1884). The young mother died one year and eight months after her son's birth. It was generally believed by the Ducasses' circle of friends that she took her own life. There is a reference to the mother-figure in the first canto of *Maldoror.*

Nothing is known about Isidore Ducasse's childhood. No document has come to light that might reveal traits and habits that developed during the first thirteen years of his life. (In his *Poésies* he clearly states that he will leave no reminiscences of his life: *je ne laisserai pas de mémoires.*) In 1856 François Ducasse was named *chancelier de première classe.* There is ample proof that he was more and more respected at the consulate. One serious insurrection that caused considerable bloodshed took place in Montevideo when

Isidore was ten. Wars and epidemics occur in *Les Chants* and might easily be magnified childhood memories.

II *Tarbes*

It was customary for emigrant families to send their sons back to France for their education. M. Ducasse followed this custom, and after the boy made his first communion, he was sent to France in 1859. The voyage lasted one month. It was the boy's first experience with what he will call *le vieil océan* and the first experience of separation from his home. This theme of a child's separation from his family is a dramatic and even a traumatic experience as it appears in the cantos.

In October 1859, Isidore Ducasse was enrolled as a boarding pupil *(interne)* in the *lycée impérial de Tarbes*. That year, at the age of thirteen, he was a member of the *classe de sixième*. He was slightly behind in his studies, but did quite well that first year at Tarbes, according to the school record. Théophile Gautier was born in Tarbes in 1811, but left at the age of three. He lived briefly in Tarbes in 1860 when Ducasse began his *lycée* years. It is curious that the *lycée* today is called *lycée* Théophile Gautier, although Gautier was never inside it, and both Isidore Ducasse and Jules Laforgue were pupils there.

The boy's first summer vacation in France was spent at the home of his uncle Marc, in the town of Bazet, five kilometers from Tarbes. In his *classe de cinquième* (1860–1861), Isidore made marked improvement in his studies, and still more improvement during the *classe de quatrième* (1861–1862). This was his last year at Tarbes. He had made a few friends during the three years: Henri Mue and Auguste Delmas, among others, and especially Georges Dazet.

A few years younger than Ducasse, this Dazet became a brilliant lawyer, first in Paris, and later in Tarbes. He played an important part in the Socialist movement, was a friend of Jules Guesde, was known for his juridical eloquence and his amorous conquests. He died in Tarbes in 1920. Georges Dazet's name heads the list of those friends to whom the *Poésies* of Lautréamont is dedicated. More than at the *lycée*, the boys' friendship probably developed during the summer vacations which Isidore spent in Bazet and Tarbes until 1867. Since he died at twenty-four, Ducasse always remained close to the intense friendships of his adolescence. The number of children and adolescents in *Les Chants de Maldoror* is one of the notable characteristics of the work, by means of which the writer preserved his own childhood.

At Tarbes, he was called by the other boys in the school *le Monté-vidéen,* somewhat to his shame, and also, still more to his discomfort, *le vampire.* There are references to the lycée experiences, notably one on the *pion* or study hall master, in *Chant I,* but the school dramas may well have been exaggerated by Lautréamont's commentators.

The home of his uncle Marc Ducasse, the oldest of eight children, provided Isidore with excellent summer vacations at Bazet, close to Tarbes, and only a few kilometers from Sarniguet, birthplace of his mother and where his father had been a schoolteacher. Bazet, a village commune of four hundred inhabitants at that time, is situated on the left bank of the Adour River. Poplars and oak trees line the river bank. The water is not deep, but like most streams in the Pyrenees it is cold and the current is swift.

The horse, which figures in *Les Chants* as one of the most often mentioned animals, was familiar to Isidore Ducasse as he grew up, first in Uruguay and then in Bazet, Sarniguet, and Tarbes where a small type of horse was bred. Horseback riding is still today a favorite sport in that part of France. Ducasse probably rode horseback almost every day in summer. On the horizon of the plain in Bazet and Tarbes, he could see the Pyrenees.

Lourdes is twenty kilometers south of Tarbes. The apparitions of the Virgin at Lourdes were recognized by the Bishop of Tarbes as early as 1858, and devotions to Notre-Dame-de-Lourdes were authorized in 1862. The Virgin is never mentioned in *Les Chants.* She is as absent from the work as the poet's mother. The name of Christ appears only once—in *Poésies.* Isidore must have received the typical religious education, first in Montevideo where he made his first communion, and then in the *lycée de Tarbes.* Throughout *Les Chants de Maldoror,* Ducasse uses all possible means to rid himself of the presence of God, and often turns his anger on priests who serve God. The passages of parody are strong examples of anticlericalism.

III *Pau*

After completing successfully his *classe de quatrième* in Tarbes, Ducasse withdrew from the *lycée* for a year during which he probably did the work of *la troisième* and *la seconde* privately or in some church institution. In October, 1863, he was in the *classe de rhétorique* in the *lycée impérial de Pau* (called today *lycée* Louis-Barthou). In a reminiscence of one of his school friends, we learn that Isidore, before entering the *lycée de Pau*, had become interested in the stories of Edgar Allen Poe. (Baudelaire had discoverd Poe just a few years earlier in 1851 and published his first translations in 1855.)

It has been surmised that the reason for the change to Pau was health. In three of the *chants* there are several references to lungs and lung trouble. It is more certain that young Ducasse suffered from serious migraine headaches. There are allusions to migraines, to insomnia, and to fever in *Les Chants*. At any rate, the *lycée de Pau* was habitually recommended to pupils whose health required an exceptionally mild and stable climate. The beauty of Pau and its site have been eloquently described by Stendhal in his *Mémoires d'un touriste*. At the time of Ducasse, the *lycée* attracted many pupils from other countries, from Spain and England in particular.

The teachers in the *classe de rhétorique* (1863–1864) were Hinstin, Zeller, and Durieux. Among Ducasse's friends were two especially, Paul Lespès and Georges Minvielle who will be remembered on the dedication page of *Poésies*. In 1928, at the age of eighty-one, Lespès reported to Alicot that he knew Ducasse better than the other students at Pau. He gave one of the very few accounts of the physical appearance of Isidore Ducasse. The boy was looked upon as strange *(fantasque)*, different from the others, irritable at times, so bold in the writing of his compositions that Professor Hinstin often had to revise the expressions. After giving a brief description of his friend as he remembered him, "tall, thin, pale, long hair falling over his forehead," Lespès spoke especially of Ducasse's interest in Professor Hinstin's classes. He was a young teacher, a Hellenist who had attended the Ecole d'Athènes, and who spoke eloquently at *lycée* graduation exercises. It would be impossible to prove that classical-sounding passages in *Les Chants* are owing to the influence of Hinstin. At times Maldoror speaks with the formulas and the tone of a teacher. Not always understood by Gustave Hinstin, and indeed often reprimanded by him, Isidore would seem to have looked upon his teacher as a surrogate father.

The following year, *la classe de philosophie* (1864–1865), Ducasse continued at Pau, without any signal success. Lespès and Minvielle remained his closest friends, although they never saw him again after that year. There is no record of Ducasse having passed his baccalaureate examinations. He left the *lycée de Pau* in August, 1865.

This was the beginning of a period in his life about which nothing is known for certain: between August, 1865, and August, 1868, when the first *chant* was published. For two years he probably lived in Tarbes or in the vicinity of Tarbes. His passport of that time classified him as "unemployed" (*sans profession*). It is likely that he was reading extensively and preparing himself for the career of a writer.

In May, 1867, Isidore Ducasse's passport bears a new visa for Montevideo, and even the name of a boat for the voyage. It seems probable that he did return at that time to Montevideo, although no absolute proof has come to light. He certainly needed to convince his father it was justifiable for him to engage upon the career of writer. The son had not seen his father for eight years. The first canto speaks of the ocean he had not seen for some time. The apostrophe to the *vieil océan* would seem to be the kind of literary piece that relates the work and the biography. The influence of Baudelaire is everywhere in *Les Chants de Maldoror,* and in the first canto, such a poem as *L'homme et la mer* is apparent. Storms at sea, the sight of the sea from the ship's deck, marine plants, sea birds, various species of large fish—all of these elements are especially to be found in Cantos I, II and IV. Literary allusions also, in addition to Baudelaire, as well as literal sea voyages account for Lautréamont's obsession with the sea. Marguerite Bonnet has pointed out his use of Michelet's *La Mer,* for example. (*La Revue d'histoire littéraire de la France,* octobre, 1964.)

If Isidore did return to Montevideo in 1867, he found his father in the old house of the rue Camacuá which had become at that time a street of prostitutes. This is related by Prudencio Montagne who, while confusing dates, did know Isidore Ducasse, although he did not realize he was interested in literature.

IV *Paris*

The actual date of Ducasse's arrival in Paris is not known. It was the end of the Empire at a time when the city architect, Haussmann, had transformed the city. For three years the young writer lived in the neighborhood of La Bourse. At the time of his death he was living in a typical *appartement meublé,* a habitation without the conveniences of a hotel and without the expansiveness of an apartment. It was the type of furnished room rented by people who stayed longer than a week or a month.

Ducasse seems to have made several friends in Paris. His publisher, Lacroix, described him as dark-haired, shaven face, tall, orderly, and industrious. His father had a banker in Paris, M. Darasse, on the rue de Lille, who provided the young man with a monthly allowance. He worked largely at night, according to Darasse's successor, and habitually declaimed in a loud voice the passage he was writing, much to the discomfort of his neighbors.

It no longer seems certain that young Ducasse came to Paris to study, presumably at the Ecole Polytechnique. At Tarbes and Pau, he had been only a fairly good student. There is no reason to believe he was an expert in mathematics. At any rate, his letters make no reference to studying. In a letter to the banker Darasse, of March 12, 1870, he wrote of sending to his father a printed preface, presumably to prove to the man in Montevideo that his son in Paris was working. Whatever money came to him from Montevideo was largely spent in publications.

The first *chant* appeared in print in November, 1868. Ducasse must have given his manuscript to the printer, Balitout, a few months earlier. The pamphlet of thirty-two pages, paid for by Ducasse, was anonymous. The name of Dazet is printed in the text. The same first canto appeared in a collection of texts by various authors, *Parfums de l'âme,* published in Bordeaux, in January, 1869. Only the initial D represented Dazet's name in this second edition. The third appearance was in the first complete edition of the six *chants de Maldoror,* brought out by Lacroix in the summer of 1869. For the first time Ducasse used the name Comte de Lautréamont. Again, the edition was subsidized by the author, and this time the name of Dazet had totally disappeared and was replaced by the names of animals. Between August, 1868, and August, 1869, Cantos II through VI were written.

The mysterious name of "Maldoror" has provoked many ingenious theories. The word would seem to be Hispanic. In Montevideo there is a street Maldonado. *Aurore* might be the dawn of life, and *mal d'aurore* (horror), the dawn without happiness. Marcel Jean and Arpad Mezei have proposed the best solution. *Mald* from *maudit* (accursed) and *oror* (*aurore* or dawn.) The accursed light would be Lucifer. Thus, *le mal d'aurore* would be reminiscent of *le mal du siècle* of the early days of Romanticism, of Alfred de Musset in particular. Like Musset in his *Confession d'un enfant du siècle,* Lautréamont, in *Les Chants de Maldoror,* is writing the story of his youth, and writing for those who suffer from the same evil or the same suffering. In *Poésies,* Lautréamont refers to Musset and warns his readers that the way opened up in *Confession d'un enfant du siècle* leads to wickedness *(méchanceté)* and lubricity.

In the work of such a young writer, the influence of earlier texts is strong, especially those who spoke of destiny: Baudelaire, Shakespeare, Goethe, Dante. Leconte de Lisle's poem "Les Hurleurs" is behind much of the eighth stanza of Canto I, the passage on the dogs howling at the moon.

At its first appearance, the *premier chant* was commented on in *La Jeunesse,* a literary magazine that was favorable to young writers. The article, signed by "Epistémon," spoke of the surprise which the reading of the work had caused. The strident hyperbole of the style, the strangeness of the narrative, the vigor of the ideas, set it apart from other works of the day. When Musset compared *la maladie du siècle* with the uncertainty of the future, the scorn of the past, the lack of religious belief and a feeling of despair, he was summarizing Romantic attitudes that easily related him to the Byronic hero and Lautréamont. Although, at its first publication, no general examination was made of the first canto, it was correctly placed by such a critic as Epistémon, in its literary tradition.

To this earliest version of the *chant,* Lautréamont brought many changes and corrections. Dazet's name disappeared, and lyric passages were rewritten with greater ferociousness.

By November, 1868, Ducasse had established relationship with the publisher Lacroix. By that time he had probably finished Canto II and begun work on Canto III. Paris, as it appears in the second canto, is still a tourist Paris, seen by a provincial or a foreigner. There is mention of the omnibus Madeleine-Bastille, of prostitution, of the age of the prostitute Maldoror meets on his daily walks, of the garden of the Tuileries (sixth stanza), of the hermaphrodites in the seventh stanza (probably seen by him in the *salle des antiques* of the Louvre), the quays along the Seine, the corpse floating in the Seine (fourteenth stanza). There is a plethora of medical terms in Canto II. One wonders if the name of imaginary creatures, Léman, Lohengrin, Hozer, represent names of new friends of Ducasse. At any rate, no proper name is exact and the keys are impossible to discover.

Canto III contains only slight biographical reference. In Canto IV there would seem to be allusions to *L'Insecte* of Michelet, first published in 1858. (It will be remembered that Canto I contains references to *La Mer* of Michelet.) Many "plagiarisms" from books of natural history were pointed out by Maurice Viroux in 1952. From the *Encyclopédie d'histoire naturelle* of Chenu, in the article on *Oiseau,* the passage on the flight of the *étourneaux* (starlings) at the beginning of Canto V, is taken without any indication of the source. Lautréamont read widely, not only the poets, but also scientific works and travel books addressed to the general public. Many of the passages he uses are not quotations but plagiarisms.

A great deal has been written about the homoerotic tendencies of Lautréamont. The stanza on the "pederasts" (Canto V) has served as the basis of most of the discussion, as proof of his homosexuality. However, it is impossible to know with certain proof his sexual practices and even his sexual proclivities. References and episodes relating to sexuality abound in *Maldoror.* The problem is always how far to accept them literally. When, for example, in Canto V, Maldoror says he does not like women *(moi, je n'aime pas les femmes),* it may be asked whether this is a clear statement of misogyny in the case of Isidore Ducasse. Maldoror immediately adds that he does not like hermaphrodites either. And yet, in Canto III, there was a lyrical passage of approval of hermaphrodites.

More important, perhaps, than these specific terms, is Maldoror's cry, often heard, of a desire to meet someone who resembles him, who possesses his nature. Such passages could signify, but not necessarily, the search for another male figure. Maldoror copulates with a shark, but it is a female shark. There are as many passages on narcissism as on homosexuality. There seem to be more passages on autoeroticism, on the practice of masturbation, or at least passages that can easily be interpreted in this way. The violently sexual episodes, such as the experiences of God in the brothel, the rape of the young girl by the shepherd dog, the fornication with the shark, might be literary borrowings from Sade. The theory of Maldoror's envy of pederasts might be offset by the total absence of any reference on the part of his friends and acquaintances to a possible inclination to sexual inversion. In *Poésies* homosexuality is specifically denied by Lautréamont.

Lautréamont indicates to the reader that there are differences between the cantos, that he changes in his attitudes toward moral problems. In Canto VI particularly, he says these differences are so marked that there is little relationship between it and the other cantos. Were the early cantos merely floundering, awkward preparations for the sixth canto and the other works that were planned?

Lautréamont worried about his power of intriguing and even hypnotizing his reader. A writer has to be read, and to achieve this, is it indispensable to write a *roman populaire* and thereby reach a vast public? He was fully aware of the sensationalism of his writings, and of its relationship with his serious professional attitude. Drawing upon popular novelists, such as Eugène Sue, and on newspaper reports on episodes of violence and scandal *(faits divers),* Lautréamont was greatly preoccupied with the suitable ways and style by which his fiction should be presented.

V   *Paris of Canto VI*

The brief story in Canto VI may be read as a parody of the *roman populaire,* but it has also an important relationship with the art of Lautréamont. The setting is no longer the Paris of Canto II, the tourist Paris, but depicts the Paris where the writer lived. It is the rue Vivienne, with its stores, gaslamps, prostitutes, the clock of the Bourse, that part of Paris that stretches between the Palais-Royal and the boulevard Montmartre. The blond hero Mervyn, after his fencing lesson, makes his way home along the big boulevards: Montmartre, Poissonnière, Bonne-Nouvelle. Then he enters the rue du Faubourg-Saint-Denis and the rue Lafayette. Mervyn's home is an up-to-date luxurious house with an inner courtyard. Even his mother's dress is described and the costumes of his young brothers. The garden of the Palais-Royal is referred to and the Place Vendôme.

In a letter to the banker Darasse, of May, 1869, Ducasse revealed a haughty attitude in speaking of money matters, an attitude that would mean he was not especially worried over the fact that the allowance money given to him by his father was diminishing. He announced that he would call for the next payment in September, three months away. Ducasse's book was published that summer, thanks to money that he had received from Darasse: *Les Chants de Maldoror,* par le comte de Lautréamont. Chants I, II, III, IV, V, VI. Paris, en vente chez tous les librairies, 1869. The name of the publisher Albert Lacroix appears in this edition as merely the printer. Since Lacroix was the publisher of Victor Hugo and Eugène Sue, Lautréamont was doubtless convinced that he would be the ideal publisher for *Maldoror.*

The choice of a pseudonym was probably advised by Ducasse's friends and by Lacroix who could easily have urged that if the young writer wished to be known, he would have to be known by a name. *Lautréamont* is beyond much doubt *Latréamont,* a novel by Eugène Sue, first published in 1838. Several theories had been advanced to explain the slight change in the first syllable of the name. Among the hypotheses, the most simple and the most probable is the faulty memory of Ducasse. He had read Eugène Sue at a very young age and failed to remember the exact spelling of the name Latréamont. He misspelled several names in the first edition of *Poésies:* Chateaubriand, Poe, Maturin, Byron, Bacon. The manuscript of *Les Chants de Maldoror* has never been found, and therefore many small problems of this nature will never be solved. Ducasse used Lautréamont only once, in this edition of Lacroix, and before his death he was using his own name for his last publications. His public today still insists on calling him Lautréamont in order to maintain the legend and the mystery surrounding Isidore Ducasse.

VI   *Publications*

Just prior to the announced publication date, in October, 1869, Lacroix decided not to release *Les Chants de Maldoror.* This last-minute decision was discussed in the Belgian bulletin devoted to works censured in France and published abroad. It was written by Auguste Poulet-Malassis, already famous for having published Baudelaire's *Les Fleurs du Mal* in 1857. In his bibliographical note,

Poulet-Malassis referred to the aesthetic of evil in Baudelaire and Flaubert, and claimed for *Maldoror* a lofty morality. Lacroix had just assumed considerable risk in publishing *Madeleine Férat* of Zola, and was aware that several passages in *Les Chants* would be material for an investigation.

So, rather than put the book on sale, he put Isidore Ducasse in contact with his Belgian associate Verboeckhaven, who made the proposal to sell the edition in Brussels. In Ducasse's answer to this proposal, he granted permission and sketched his aesthetics as a defense of his book. He put himself in the category of other writers who had used evil as a theme: Byron, Milton, Musset, Baudelaire. Ducasse accepted the financial conditions of the Belgian publisher. In February, 1870, he was still writing to Verboeckhaven about his edition which had not yet appeared. In a letter of February 21, he announced an important change in his writing, a denial of his past, and a new theme of hope *(J'ai renié mon passé. Je ne cherche plus que l'espoir)*. This was an announcement of *Poésies,* a manuscript he planned to take to Lacroix in March. He still owed Lacroix eight hundred francs from the earlier contract.

In March, Lautréamont was living at 15, rue Vivienne, close to the spot where rue Colbert crosses it and where Maldoror waited for Mervyn to pass *(Chant* VI). There are several matters of importance in his letter of March 12 to Darasse: a review of his former work, which had not yet appeared, which had cost twelve hundred francs and of which he had paid only four hundred, his dislike of the typical Romantic lament over life, the weak attitudes of Lamartine, Hugo and Musset, and his new style of writing, his new method that sings of hope, happiness, and duty. This new work (to be called *Poésies*) will be completed in four or five months. He needs an advance in money to pay for the printing of the preface which he intends to send to his father in Montevideo, in order to prove to him that he is working.

The preface referred to was *Poésies I.* It is likely that at that time both *Poésies I* and *II* were written. Actually a few sentences in the letter were taken from the work itself. This letter to his banker is Lautréamont's only explanation of his work that we have. The banker carried out the young writer's request.

When the first unit of *Poésies* was submitted in April to the Ministry of the Interior, Isidore Ducasse signed his own name as the author. This use of his name would seem to correspond to the authenticity of his new writing, to a conviction that it reflected his real personality. The title did not refer to "poetry" in a narrow sense, but to "literature" in a general sense. The publication was a brochure of sixteen pages, and the printer was again Balitout, Questroy, 7, rue Baillif. There was a long list of dedicatees, twelve names of friends and acquaintances, beginning with the name of Georges Dazet and ending with Monsieur Hinstin, the *professeur de rhétorique* of Pau.

A critical tone is more apparent in *Poésies,* and the young author of twenty-four seems to be denying his *Chants* or at least regretting the literary influences that were apparent in *Les Chants.* The passions themselves should not be described, says Lautréamont, but they should be seen from a moral viewpoint. This new critical or scientific attitude he calls *poésie.* This professorial tone had also been apparent in *Les Chants.* Lautréamont had not performed as radical a change as he believed. The two parts of *Poésies* form an adjunct to *Maldoror* rather than its negation. The new work is not a direct change or rejection, but rather a commentary in which the narrative elements of *Les Chants* are modified and altered into a more aphoristic critical compendium.

Poésies has its own interest for readers today, despite the harsh comment of Albert Camus who, in *L'homme révolté,* declares it to be of a *banalité absolue.* Far from appearing as a contradiction, it appears now as a critical assessment of a young writer's powers.

The second fascicule of *Poésies* was printed by Balitout and placed in the Ministry of the Interior between the 18th and 25th of June. On the dedication page, rather than the names of the first fascicule, appears

Le Gérant

I.D.

rue du Faubourg-Montmartre, 7

This is the last address of Ducasse. Four addresses in three years were not excessive for that type of lodging, the furnished apartment.

It is not known whether the two brochures were distributed. The first half of July was a period of momentous days in Paris, ending with the declaration of war on July 19. *Poésies* was advertised in *La Revue Populaire de Paris* in the July issue.

VII *War*

On September 2nd, Napoleon III capitulated at Sedan. On September 8th, the Ministry of the Interior announced that the enemy was advancing on Paris. On the 16th, Victor Hugo, who had just returned to Paris from his long self-imposed exile, sent out an appeal to the French to prepare to oppose the invaders. The siege of Paris began in October and continued through November and December. Paris was bombarded every day in January, 1871. The

LAUTRÉAMONT

CHAPTER 3

Les Chants de Maldoror

I Canto I

COMPOSED of fourteen parts or stanzas, the introductory canto is memorable for the ninth, the elaborate apostrophe to the ocean which offers one of the principal keys to the work as a whole. It is a hymn to the ocean as source of everything, as the symbol of man's history in its perpetuity and invariableness.

Of the eight stanzas preceding this epic-like salutation, the first five are brief, and each one is on a different theme. These five themes are interrelated and are quite specifically those themes the most often repeated and analyzed throughout the work. They are followed by three stanzas which are scenes—episodes of violence that announce in their own way the kind of experience that Maldoror will observe or conduct. The five stanzas that follow the ocean apostrophe, combine the statement-like stanza of a theme with a partially developed scene of action.

Stanza 1. The opening sentence establishes a relationship with the reader by announcing the hardness and terror of the pages to come, and the need for the reader to be equally hardened to and attracted to what creates terror in man. The first words are both incitement and warning. The book is dangerous and is addressed only to those few readers who are able to understand why they take perverse delight in the depiction of danger. As Dante warned those entering hell, and as Baudelaire advised the ordinary reader to reject his book, so Lautréamont clears the way for only the stouthearted among his readers.

The rest of the stanza is an image—the flight of cranes *(grues)* in the sky as they form an angle. The oldest crane, the leader, who flies in the foremost point of the angle, suddenly senses danger ahead. It is a storm perhaps. His cry, in his role of sentinel, causes the form of the perfectly shaped angle to break. The cranes follow the leader and take another route. This bird-augury demonstrates a lesson to the timid reader and also reminds all readers that we have in us deep primordial instincts, as deep as the instinct of a bird that directs his flight through the sky. This beautifully fashioned introduction leads us back to the beginning of time.

Stanza 2. Another single paragraph, shorter still than the first, asks the reader if he wants hate *(la haine)* to be invoked. Sensual man, like a shark turning on its stomach in the water, is a monster living with God's curse, because hate provides voluptuousness, and the satisfaction that comes from a knowledge of evil. Baudelaire, without being named, seems insistently present in these opening passages.

Stanza 3. Maldoror is introduced in the opening sentence. In very few words his biography is summarized. He was happy during his early years, until he realized he was born evil. With that realization of his fate, he embarked upon a career of evil. It would be impossible for him to do otherwise. The word evil *(mal)* forms the first syllable of his name. The other two syllables *(doror)* might be *d'aurore,* evil from the beginning, from dawn.

Stanza 4. Isn't there a strong relationship between genius and cruelty? A leading question serves as introduction to what follows. The delight of cruelty *(les délices de la cruauté)* seems to summarize the goal to be reached. The final sentence of the stanza, stating that the wickedest thoughts of the hero of this work are in all men, is a reminder of the intimacy between writer and reader.

Stanza 5. This last introductory stanza, announcing themes and warnings, is almost an episode, almost a picture of the hero in action. But here he represents the past that historically preceded his life. Unable to laugh normally, Maldoror cut with a penknife *(un canif)* the two sides of his mouth, and even then his laughter was not human. How could he be? He is too conscious of all the evil acts of men who came before him, and he lists acts of dishonor and cruelty. The tone is biblical and indeed Maldoror alludes to the Old Testament flood sent by God to destroy the world in its wickedness. But this divine act was to no avail. Men easily forget and their evil ways start up again with almost no interruption. He invokes the blue firmament, the sea, the land, the inhabitants of all the spheres, the entire universe. And then, addressing God who created it all, asks God to show him a single man who is good!

Stanza 6. This passage, close in form to an episode, is at least a fragmentary scene in which Lautréamont describes a paradox of man's behavior, one that follows logically the abrupt question that ended Stanza 5. It is man's capacity to inflict pain or suffering on a being he loves. This act is followed by an effort, seemingly sincere, to console and placate and restore the one tortured. The general example of a child victim is replaced by the example of an adolescent who is blindfolded and who therefore does not know that his torturer is the same man who consoles him afterward, who licks his wounds and who kisses him on the mouth in an act of love. The criminal asks pardon of the adolescent now maimed for life. The boy is compared to Jesus whose power of forgiveness was infinite. The New Testament allusion, coming after the Old, seems to name the torturer as apostle and thus accentuates the endlessness of evil in every man.

Stanza 7. This episode opens with a bravura-like statement: Maldoror has made a pact with prostitution in order to sow discord in families. Used as a sermon text, the first sentence leads into a tomb scene with elements that recall Dante's *Inferno,* although no one specific passage is used. A huge firefly *(ver luisant)* calls attention to the inscription which Maldoror reads: "Here lies an adolescent. Do not pray for him." A naked woman crouches at Maldoror's feet. Again, the *ver luisant* conducts the scene. He calls the woman *prostitution* and orders Maldoror to kill her. He raises a large rock, climbs a mountain, and from there crushes the firefly. The word *ver* recalls the first syllable of Vergil, Dante's guide in the underworld. Maldoror is evidently to remain alone. He tells the woman he prefers her to the firefly because he pities the wretched, and that henceforth the winter wind over the sea and cities will be the mingled sigh of prostitution and the groaning of the Montevidean. Maldoror's pact with prostitution seems to represent an analogy with Jesus' gentle treatment of the prostitute.

Stanza 8. The scene shifts to one of trees and moonlight and a countryside. Yellow forms move about here and there, adding to the eeriness of the tableau. The hooting of an owl and the moaning of the wind incite the dogs of the farms to break their chains and run about wild. Their barking resembles or stands for the sounds made by mankind when terrorized: a hungry child, a woman giving birth, a dying man. They bark *at* (*contre* in the French text) everything in the universe: the stars, the moon, the mountains, the cold air, the silence of night, owls, hares, thieves, snakes, trees, spiders, crows, rocks. They bark at huge fish when they rise to the surface of the sea, and at men who are their masters. Their rage is endless because they long for the infinite. When Maldoror compares himself to the dogs, we realize this is a passage on the atavistic traits of man, traits we derive from animals and all living things. Like the dogs, Maldoror is a night prowler. His rage is related to the rabies of a dog. This is the real setting for Maldoror's drama. His rage is in the long litany of phrases with the preposition *contre*. His thirst *(soif)* for God accounts for his rage. He is against all creation and all incomprehensible things.

Stanza 9. This apostrophe or solemn hymn to the ocean breaks out with words stressing its seriousness and coldness: *je me propose de déclamer à grande voix la strophe sérieuse et froide que vous allez entendre*. It is both a salutation, *je te salue, vieil océan*, and the history of man whose real nature is oceanic. This nature, abiding and imperturbable and vast, is the subconscious. Lautréamont is going to invoke the subconscious throughout *Les Chants de Maldoror* by means of oceans and vessels, storms at sea and sea monsters, half-concealed reefs and shipwrecks. The ocean is the symbol of identity in its invariableness:

> *Vieil océan, tu es le symbole de l'identité:*
> *toujours égal à toi-même.*

The ocean depths are comparable to the depths of the heart. The celibacy of the ocean *(Vieil océan, ô grand célibataire!)* implies the promiscuousness of man's nature, the waves of passion that break over him and disappear. The subconscious of man, that part of his nature that remembers everything, is therefore oceanic, and his conscious nature is terrestrial.

The sea also is maternal *(la mer, la mère)*. The basic Freudian complex is apparent in *Les Chants* when the child encounters first his parents and where his sexual interest is first fixed on one of the parents, according to his sex: the son who will hate his father and love his mother; and the daughter who will love her father and hate her mother. God, the symbol of the father, is ceaselessly attacked throughout all six cantos. In the sea imagery of the mother is described the prenatal life of the child. It is the appropriate introduction to the life story of the epic hero Maldoror. In the final apostrophe, *Vieil océan, ô grand célibataire,* Maldoror asks whether the ocean is the dwelling place of the Prince of Darkness.

Stanza 10. In the strong opening sentence, Maldoror announces that he will allow no priests to be present at his bedside when he dies. For the scene of his death he will choose a stormy sea or a mountaintop so that he will merge with the void. He imagines the scene from which he will observe acts of human wickedness and where he will be seen by the eagle, the crow, the pelican, the wild duck, and the migrating crane. The litany-like lists of animals only serve to accent the aloneness of Maldoror. After speaking of the solitude of death, he speaks of his separation from all men, and calls upon the wind to elevate him away from the earth and the perfidiousness of men. This is the saddest of the stanzas.

Stanza 11. This long scene of fiction is close to the form of the Gothic tale or such a work as *Les mystères de Paris* of Eugène Sue. (We remember that one of Sue's heroes is Latréamont.) It is a scene on the eeriness and the sinister play of evil. Maldoror has simply to look at a family scene in the evening, mother and father and their obedient young son, to disturb the peace and to change the happiness into disaster. Without literally seeing Maldoror, they all suddenly feel his presence, and know it to be an evil presence. Outside, at a great distance, the cry of the vampire is heard. Edouard, the son, gradually feels the seduction of the stranger, and his parents plead with him never to imitate this man. At first he struggles against the mysterious force in him that is alienating him from his home and from all that is familiar. But the boy finally succumbs to the spell cast over him. His death at the end of the stanza seems more symbolic than literal. At the end of Canto VI a similar scene of seduction will be enacted in greater detail and realism.

Stanza 12. In *Hamlet*, the gravediggers are traditionally played as clowns joking about death. Their remarks form a striking contrast with the somber thoughts by Hamlet himself. But in this episode of Lautréamont, the gravedigger *(le fossoyeur)* is oppressed by death and by his considerations of the soul's immortality or mortality. Maldoror, in Norway, goes to a cemetery, talks with a gravedigger and consoles him concerning the harassing problems of existence. While he helps dig the grave, the gravedigger begins to wonder who this stranger is. Is he a dispossessed monarch? Out of pity, the gravedigger offers him the hospitality of his hut, as, in Byron's poem, the hunter offered Manfred the shelter of his chalet.

Stanza 13. Lautréamont is closer here to Milton than to Dante or Baudelaire or Byron. At the beginning of *Paradise Lost,* Satan announces that his delight is to do evil. This thought is often repeated by Maldoror when he speaks of his career of evil and the delight of cruelty. Satan appears to Maldoror, at first at some distance, in the form of a toad *(un crapaud).* The Miltonic-like description is detailed: monstrous eyes, huge eyelids, a more than human figure, this monarch of ponds and swamps. The toad speaks and advises Maldoror to leave this planet and return to the spheres from which he came. The toad's words are not unlike Satan's speech in *Paradise Lost* to the angels who had remained faithful to God.

Stanza 14. After thirteen stanzas stressing the inheritance—intellectual and psychic—of Maldoror, we come to the end of Canto I when the actual birth of Lautréamont is announced as taking place at the mouth of the Plata where Buenos Aires and Montevideo look at one another across the Argentine waters of the estuary.

II   Canto II

The second canto is largely on infancy and childhood. Evil is in man from the very beginning. This is the longest and most varied canto, with sixteen stanzas, and appropriately so, because the principal traits of a man's personality are fixed during early childhood. In keeping with the epic tradition as well as the psychoanalytic tradition, episodes of the hero's childhood are related, and they are all episodes of violence: either violence observed, as in scenes of paternal anger, or violence perpetrated in scenes of infantile sadism or plottings of murder.

Stanza 1. Someone (Lautréamont presumably) is speaking to man throughout this stanza, and telling him that he is made up especially of evil. His place in the universe is where he belongs and where he will end. The voice seems almost paternal. Man has no need to complain. This is as it is.

Stanza 2. Lautréamont feels a great need to write and yet his fingers are paralyzed. A wild storm outside seems to be related to this paralysis of his hand. The blood that is everywhere . . . on the floor, on shirts and handkerchiefs, comes from the arteries of Maldoror. The need to clean the room and hide traces of the blood is perhaps related to the need to write, which might well be the need to masturbate. The loss of blood would be therefore sperm in onanistic practice. The gratuitous spilling of blood, of which there are so many examples in *Les Chants de Maldoror,* would seem to be masturbation as in this stanza where blood comes from self-inflicted punishments as well as punishments meted out to a child from someone else.

Stanza 3. This is a close continuation of Stanza 2, where Maldoror makes plans to kill his friend Lohengrin by using a dagger that is carefully described in phallic terms. The plan to kill without reason could be equated with a sexual drive. Lohengrin and Maldoror, portrayed as friends, would be the same boy, if the experience as described here under the direction of God, is masturbation.

Stanza 4. The hallucinatory fourth stanza scene of the omnibus that goes between the Bastille and the Madeleine Church, shows a group of people resembling a family, comfortably seated in the omnibus, impervious to a wretched child of eight who implores help as he stands on the street. Lautréamont asks if this is human charity and denounces the race of man: *race stupide et idiote.* The child in this episode would seem to represent the fate of a lonely individual ignored and even oppressed by society. The indifference of man with regard to other men is a theme somewhat associated with Kafka. The travelers in the omnibus do not hear the cries of the child because each one is lost in his own solitude. The child calling after the omnibus is the anguish of the adolescent trying to discover his past, his relationship with adults, and his effort to recover from a sense of alienation. The scene in its intensity is comparable to a Baudelaire prose poem in *Spleen de Paris*.

Stanza 5. It is not clear whether the girl Maldoror encounters in his walks through the city is a prostitute or not. But his imagination makes her into that. He is perhaps trying to justify (as a young boy might) his lack of strong attraction to the girl. And so he invents an outrageous punishment for her by whirling her around him like a slingshot and hurling her against a wall. This scene will be recapitulated in greater detail at the end of the work. It is another chapter on Lautréamont's disgust with mankind. After the omnibus scene with its picture of dehumanized society, here is a reference to prostitution which makes man's solitude seem even more implacable.

Stanza 6. This is the picture of an innocent child seated on a bench in the Tuileries Garden where Maldoror is initiating him, by speech, to the evils of the world. Two words with sexual overtones, one at the beginning, *équivoques,* and the other, at the end, *passion,* lead one to believe that the speech is that of the seducer, of the man initiating the boy into sexual practices. At the end of the stanza, the boy is certainly aroused and eager to play a dominant role, whether in life in general or in sexuality. The actual words of Maldoror and the boy closely resemble the words of Vautrin to young Eugène de Rastignac in *Le Père Goriot*. The lesson given to Maldoror is one known to succeed in the world: a young boy who hasn't the strength of a man can succeed if he is wily enough: *sois le plus rusé*. The shepherd boy David, thanks to ruse and clever plotting, overcame the giant Goliath.

Stanza 7. This passage, on the hermaphrodite, is a lyrical interval, an evocation of a beautiful figure half-male, half-female, sleeping in a grove. He is attacked and beaten by four masked men. After this lesson of violence, the hermaphrodite persists in remaining alone, in refusing the advances of the world, in living completely within a narcissistic dream for himself. This phase of self-love is a protection from the world's hostility, and Lautréamont does not hesitate to urge reclusion and sleep and separation from the world's ferocity:

*Ne te réveille pas, hermaphrodite ... Dors, dors toujours ...
n'ouvre pas les yeux.* Twentieth-century critics, Albert Béguin
and Mircea Eliade, among others, have pointed out the importance
of the theme of the hermaphrodite or the androgen in Romanticism
(Gautier in *Mlle de Maupin,* for example) and Symbolism. In the
life cycle of Maldoror, this is the moment of bisexuality that pre-
cedes the discovery of the true nature of a boy's sexuality. A bucolic
moment in the midst of episodes that are far from bucolic.

Stanza 8. The repulsiveness of this stanza is realistic and deliberate
and Dantesque. The young child is growing in innocence and
beauty. He is angelic until one day he has a vision of God. It is a
terrifying vision in which God is eating the dead body of a human
being. Other bodies are floating in a huge chamber pot full of
human excrement. Whenever God wants to eat, he simply pulls
another body out of the receptacle. This scene of revelation marks
a profound change in the boy. According to the narration of
Lautréamont, he suddenly hears for the first time a *sound.* The
picture of Dante's Satan is replaced by God, an anthropophagic
god. Paintings of Goya come to mind, and stories of ogres. But
especially scenes from *The Inferno:* The episode of Ugolino
(Canto 32) biting into the skull of Ruggieri; and the eighteenth
canto where sinners are plunged in human excrement. Two reminiscences of Dante are quite explicit. The boy is tired from climbing
(Un jour, donc, fatigué de talonner du pied ...) and looks
up at a bluish circle of light in the sky. It is the opening passage
of Canto I. And especially the passage where the boy is so emotionally
upset that he almost falls backward three times. At several points
during his descent through hell, Dante falls because of this feeling
of pity or terror.

This scene of God the father could be a scene of sexuality between
his father and mother observed by a child. This is often of such a
shocking nature to a boy that he will feel impotent for a long time
thereafter, and harbor a feeling of resentment toward his parents.

Stanza 9. This amazing story of lice is one of the hardest to
interpret. It is an invocation to the power of lice to multiply so
rapidly that they can set up their own régime and control the world.
Lautréamont imagines a reign, a dynasty so powerful that he would

have to rise above the earth on angel wings in order to contemplate the spectacle. In the life story of the hero this episode is puberty and the multiplying lice are the spermatozoa, the sexual excess of the boy who is amazed at the power of his fertility. The daily repetitive onanistic practices of a boy, the waste of sperm and the obsession with sperm are transcribed by the nightmare about lice and their domination of the world. When a peasant sees a meteor fall from the sky and crash into a cornfield, he will now know that it was Maldoror hurling from on high a block of lice to pollute the world. This image of the meteor is aptly chosen to describe the orgasm of the youth.

Stanza 10. The tenth stanza that solemnly begins with the words, *O mathématiques sévères, je ne vous ai pas oubliées,* and that is in a literal sense an apostrophe to mathematics, to its power and splendor, to the services it renders mankind, has more clues than the lice stanza to its symbolic meaning. It would seem to be a passage on the hero's mother, the first development of the Oedipus complex, in which mathematics is called the source and the fortifying milk which the hero drinks. Mathematics, or the mother, appears as chaos out of whose entrails a treasure will be brought forth. The multiplication of cells during the period of gestation is implied in the choice of this symbol, and supplementary images, pyramids, and labyrinths reinforce the image of the maternal womb in whose darkness the hero first discovered the meaning of evil:

> *Le premier, je découvris, dans les ténèbres*
> *de ses entrailles, ce vice néfaste, le mal!*

The maternal image, in its sacred imperturbable manifestation of mathematics, is the consolation for the wickedness of man and the injustice of God. This is the ultimate sentence of the stanza, the ultimate exhortation: *O mathématiques saintes!*

Stanza 11. As might be expected, this stanza following the apostrophe to mathematics with its emphasis on the maternal image, is on the hero's relationship to the father, which is basically the Oedipus complex of hatred for the father. And here again, Lautréamont has invented an intriguing image to designate the father, and a scene of violence to designate the son's murder of the father.

The hero is watching a silver lamp in a cathedral. It shines in the dark colonnades of the basilica as if it were choosing its victims among the kneeling penitents. The lamp so irritates Maldoror that he wishes it would turn into a man so that he could attack it. The wish is granted and the lamp turns into the figure of an angel. A fight ensues and Maldoror strangles the Lord's emissary.

Stanza 12. With the twelfth stanza we have reached the hero's age of puberty when the prayers he had learned as a child sadden and irritate him because he is learning another kind of prayer, the offering up of himself in the practice of onanism. Many elements in the stanza point to this as the new experience for the boy: the tormenting dreams he has, the rights that his nature claims, his feelings that repeatedly lead him to this inclination *(vers cette pente).* The other boys around him are having the same experience which he contrasts with the sterile repetition of his childish prayers. Masturbation would be the parody of a child's prayer *(chaque jour, j'éléverai vers toi les accents de mon humble prière)* as well as the imitation of the father *(tel père, tel fils)* which is in the preceding stanza.

Stanza 13. Again, in logical sequence, the thirteenth, an elaborate episode of action, is the narrative of Maldoror's first love *(mon premier amour,* he calls it in the last words of the stanza) or rather his first sexual experience after the practice of masturbation. This is one of the most powerful and shocking passages in *Les Chants de Maldoror.* In order to depict incest in the life story of Maldoror, the hero's first knowledge of sexual love, which will be with his mother, in keeping with the ancient myth of Oedipus, Lautréamont imagines the hero seated on a rock near the sea. He watches a storm rise up and a ship strike against a reef and sink. He watches the death agony of the shipwrecked passengers with a sadistic voluptuousness. Six sharks swim into the mêlée and devour the survivors. A huge female shark then enters the fray and kills three of the sharks. Maldoror shoots another of the monsters and then, armed with a knife, leaps into the water. Maldoror and the female shark easily destroy the two remaining sharks, and then begin in the water an amazing scene of admiration and veneration. They embrace tenderly and then unite sexually. The union is pure and hideous, and the hero no longer feels alone. He is face to face with his first love. This is the act of incest in the life story of the hero. Since the ocean is the mother image, the female shark symbolizes the mother, and the union of the son and the mother takes place in the ocean depths:

> *vers les profondeurs de l'abîme, ils se*
> *réunirent dans un accomplissement long,*
> *chaste et hideux!*

The act is described as the accomplishment of a primordial instinct of humanity. The shark and the young man are attracted to one another like two magnets:

> *ils tombèrent brusquement l'un contre*
> *l'autre, comme deux aimants.*

There are many examples of storms at sea and shipwrecks in nine-teenth-century adventure novels. The picture of a single figure escaping from a shipwreck and struggling against the ocean is re-peated in Canto IV, Stanza 6. A similar scene is in Byron's *Manfred*. The joining of the female shark with Maldoror might have been suggested by a passage on the love life of sharks in Michelet's *La Mer*. This shark scene was often singled out for commentary by early readers of Lautréamont, notably by Huysmans.

Stanza 14. It is a Paris scene, reminiscent in many ways of a Baudelaire prose poem. The drowning body of a young man in the Seine is seen floating down the river, turning over with the current, and finally caught by a boatman at the end of his pole. The body is stretched out on the bank. The curious bystanders look at him, talk about him and discuss the art of suicide, but they do not touch him or help revive him for fear of appearing softhearted. Maldoror comes by on horseback. He stops, gets down from his horse, empties the body of water, massages the young man and breathes into his mouth. After an hour's work, life returns to the boy and at the same time a rejuvenation covers the face of Maldoror. The rescuer, called here "the man with bronze lips" *(l'homme aux lèvres de bronze)* recognizes in the revived body his friend Holzer. The two embrace and ride off together on the horse. Thus the theme of suicide and self-destruction is offset by the expression of friendship which by its staged dramatic revival and by its effusiveness may be a sexual friendship.

Stanza 15. The suicide attempt of Stanza 14 was among the last typical experiences in the life story of a youth. He has now reached the moment when he has to examine his conscience and listen to its voice. The images describing Maldoror's conscience are all violent and melodramatic. At first, the conscience is a ghost pursuing Maldoror through a stormy night. The night itself opens like the lips of a dark vagina out of which flow a river of sperm. A man's conscience tracks him down like a fox at night. A mysterious passage seems to make the Creator Maldoror's conscience, and the two are described as neighboring monarchs *(deux monarques voisins)*, each fully aware of his own power, and each unable to win definitively over the other. The conscience then assumes a human form and Maldoror gnaws at its skull. (It is a Dante image already used in the eighth stanza of this canto.)

When Maldorer, locked with his conscience, hurls himself into the void, he releases the conscience that falls hard against the pavement below, while he like a bird descends slowly. Once on the ground again, he goes toward a guillotine, severs the heads of three young girls, and then attempts to have his own head cut off. But the blade does not cut into his neck. He is invulnerable and walks away applauded by the crowd. This extermination of Maldoror's conscience is a listing of extraordinary feats. His power is limitless because these are imagined victories over all the forces that thwart his development. He frees himself by the magic of dreams and fantasies. He exists now without his conscience.

Stanza 16. In just a few lines, Lautréamont concludes Canto II. He stops and looks back as if he were looking into the vagina of a woman, as if he were contemplating all the experiences he has narrated, beginning with that of his birth. His exploration, momentarily at least, has come to an end. And he is hardened now. His skin is that of a crocodile.

III Canto III

If the book is read as the life story of a man resembling the epic hero, Canto III might be interpreted as the initiation to life, following

Canto I where some stanzas seem to relate a prenatal or uterine life, and Canto II where important stanzas are clearly related to childhood.

Stanza 1. The opening stanza is mysterious and composed in a style which now is recognizably Lautréamont's. Two brothers are riding horseback side by side. Might they be the two selves of Maldoror, the male and the female principles of the hero? The first initiation of the hero had been the separation from the mother, the emergence from the sea *(source, mère)*, and the first experience on the solid earth. In terms of the entire work, the two brothers would be the subconscious *(la mer)* and the conscious *(la terre)* which now exist side by side as the two horses gallop along the shore. During the ride they experience a premonition of disaster, a vision of life as being a wound: *j'ai reçu la vie comme une blessure.* The stanza is an epic-like passage of movement and speed, a prelude to the battle announcing the ferociousness of the second stanza.

The first stanza begins with the recall of four names from the second canto: Léman, Lohengrin, Lombano, Holzer. Are they angelic imaginary beings, as the poet calls them, companions of Maldoror, or are they names covering the real names of Lautréamont's friends, or are they quite simply projections of fantasies, idealized adolescents? It is a curious litany of names of figures who developed into characters of his mind and who made their way into his writing. It is an apostrophe to the heroes, to those beings who inhabit our memory and our subconscious, out of whom a real fictional hero may be fabricated if the fantasies are recast in writing.

As soon as they are named, Lautréamont tells us he allowed them to fall back into the chaos of the subconscious, into the void: *je vous ai laissés retomber dans le chaos.* But the following sentence is dominated by the verb *enfanter.* His love will "engender" these beings and others. His love is described as thirsting for the human race. It is the picture of the solitary writer explaining the genesis of his writing, of his need to relive his fantasies and recreate them in his new role of demiurge. The "hole of hell" *(la cave de l'enfer),* or lost consciousness, is juxtaposed with a garland of camellias *(guirlande de camélias)* or the resurrection in art of what has been forgotten.

When the narrative of the ride is resumed, Mario is named as the companion rider, the setting of beaches is described, and the wind ruffles up the hair of the two riders. A sea gull *(la mouette)* by its cry warns of a storm, and a lonely fisherman wonders about the "two mysterious brothers," as he watches them gallop past. He hides in fear of them. Maldoror (or Lautréamont) is indeed in this scene the terrifying demiurge, separated from ordinary men. This is the way legends begin: apparitions at the time of disaster. The two horsemen are phantom riders whose black wings allow them to mount into the sky. They are called by the author-interpreter the genie of the earth and the genie of the sea. Like two condors over the Andes, they are united in eternal friendship. The concentric circles they describe in the air give a sense of supernatural order by comparison with the revolutions and calamities taking place on the surface of the land. They are above the cruelty of men engaged in battle or in killing one another secretly with a knife.

The two riders are thus compared to those beings who inhabit regions at a great distance from the world of men: a planetary world, a volcano, an underground seething cauldron. Their words and their prophesies go unheeded by the earthbound.

Mario and Maldoror, angel of the earth and angel of the sea, gallop along the coast. They grow closer to one another. Yet fear intercepts their union, either a physical or sentimental union. As the Gothic-supernatural elements increase in this opening stanza, so does the union of the two riders become more intense, but it is always under the domination of the Almighty. The sentimental relationship is given more and more human characteristics as the mythic elements grow. Both the conclusion and the explanation of the passage are the key sentence of Maldoror saying he received life as a wound, and his desire to have the Creator see his distress and his scar. The galloping of the horses along the banks of the sea is heard in the last sentence.

Stanza 2. The swift movement of the first stanza, with its predictions of gloom and wrath and violence in man's struggle with God, and especially with its almost final word of wound *(blessure),* prepares the sadism of the second stanza. It is a scene closely modeled on a typical episode in the novels of Sade, where Maldoror brutally attacks a little girl who is then raped by a bulldog. The pornography is traditional and the physiological details of the passage would be those chosen by a writer of pornography to stimulate his readers.

The narration is presented in a traditional manner. A madwoman, pursued by children who are throwing stones at her, is described in detail. Her mind has gone and her beauty also. She refuses to speak of the disasters that caused her downfall, but one day she drops a roll of paper, the manuscript in which the story is written. This manuscript narrative occupies most of the stanza. When the woman's daughter is born, after years of sterility, she gives thanks to God for the blessing. She devotes her life to her child, and answers as best she can the questions of a child about life and death, about animals and flowers.

The child began to wander off alone, as she followed the birds and picked flowers. When the drama happened, the mother was not present. The story was told to her. Maldoror with his bulldog passed by, saw the girl, took off his clothes and raped her. He put on his clothes and then ordered his dog to strangle the girl. But the dog misunderstood the order, and copied his master by raping the child a second time. The horrors of the scene continue, when Maldoror cuts an eyeball of the dog who runs off dragging the body of the girl who had not been separated from the dog. The body finally drops to the ground where Maldoror attacks it again, this time opening the vagina with a knife and pulling out the various organs of the child.

A shepherd who had witnessed the crime, told of it long after he was sure the assassin had fled. The ending of the story is the attitude of the mother toward the murderer of her daughter. She pitied him if he had lost his reason and was insane when committing the crime. But she pitied him also if his mind was intact because his behavior concealed such a deep hate for mankind.

Stanza 3. This stanza is briefer than the second. It is in the form of another narrative, and marks a decisive moment in the career of Maldoror. The stanza opens with the name of a new character, Tremdall, who is the observer of an epic fight between a dragon and an eagle. The young man is standing over a valley and sees from a distance a dragon, larger than an oak tree, climbing up one side of the valley, in search of Maldoror. In order to engage in such a deadly battle, Maldoror changes himself into a huge eagle.

The two winged monsters circle around one another, each time coming closer. The dragon seems the stronger of the two, and Tremdall hopes the dragon will win. The dragon begins the fight with a blow of his claw. The eagle gouges out an eye of his enemy with his beak. Tremdall is intoxicated with the sight of the wounds as they accumulate. The eagle is more prudent, more astute than the dragon, and at the end, covered with blood, he attaches himself on the body of the dragon, as if he were a bloodsucker, and with his beak makes wound after wound in the neck and belly of his enemy.

Maldoror is victim. With the issue of this fight, he begins his career of evil *(la carrière du mal)*. He has slain hope and henceforth will feed on despair. He recovers his human form, and as he flees into the distance, Tremdall recognizes him as being damned and as one who curses others. . . . Thus in the life story of this hero, an important decision has been reached which will help to explain the rest of the narrative. Maldoror has gone over to the side of evil. He will be representative and active in the cause of evil.

Quite appropriately, because of this decision, Stanzas 4 and 5 are given over to a depicting, which is in reality a denunciation, of God the Father. The argument would seem to be that since God is the creator of the universe and of everyone and everything in it, he is therefore the creator of vices.

Stanza 4. This stanza is brief and serves as an introduction to the longer Stanza 5. A day in spring provides an idyllic setting for the happiness and harmony of birds and trees and human beings. Every element of the universe has accepted its destiny. Except the Creator himself! He is represented as a loathsome filthy human figure. His blond hair reminds the reader that almost all the young men in *Les Chants* are described as blond . . .

This figure of God has collapsed on the roadside through drunkenness. He is as drunk as a bedbug *(une punaise)* that had drunk three barrels of blood during the night. Most of the stanza is a parade of birds and animals who pass by a prostrated figure of God, and harass him in a physical sense: the heron, the owl, the donkey, the toad, and many others. The lion speaks of God's greatness which now appears in eclipse. He derides the lesser animals for tormenting God when he is in a drunken stupor. Finally a man passes by and for three days lets fall his excrement on the august face. Up until this final episode, the passage resembles a fable of La Fontaine.

Then God bestirs himself, rises and sits on a rock. The author here seems to intervene and warns his fellowmen to show some respect to the Almighty. He reminds us that it is not easy to hold the reins of the universe, that sheer fatigue can lead astray even God himself.

Stanza 5. The entire canto has been a preparation for the final scene in this stanza, the longest of the entire work. It is a scene of debauchery in a bordello where the hero (Maldoror? Lautréamont?) encounters God (or his father?) who is depicted as the supreme profligate. This is the lowest, the most shameful initiation to life that Lautréamont was able to conceive: the vilification of the father (or of God), the one to whom the hero owes his life. Outside the building, an inscription on a pillar of a bridge, in Hebrew letters, warns the passerby not to enter. It has the ring of Dante's warning over the gate of hell *(Voi ch'entrate): Vous, qui passez sur ce pont, n'y allez pas.*

The real horror and strangeness of a Dante-like scene begins when the hero is in the room and sees what he believes to be a blond stick *(un bâton blond)* moving about and walking. He compares it to a battering ram *(un bélier)* striking against the gates of a besieged city, or to an eel *(anguille)* because of its suppleness and capacity to take different forms. On closer examination, the moving object is seen to be a hair *(un cheveu)* which, when it speaks, says it had fallen from the head of his master when he had combed his hair after rising from the bed in this house of prostitution.

The obviously phallic object speaks of his abandonment in the room, and the hero wonders who this master could be. He listens attentively to the explanation of the hair. During the night of orgy between his master and the prostitute, he felt he was becoming detached at the root and fell like a dead branch from the illustrious head. The narrative is at regular intervals interrupted by the litany-like phrase repeated by the hero: "I wondered who his master could be!" The hair describes the most sensual aspects of the lovemaking— the master smelling the armpits and the nostrils of the woman, for example. At one moment, he wanted to engage in sadistic acts, and rather than perpetrate them on the woman, he seized a young man in an adjoining room, who had come there to see a prostitute. The hair, stretched out on the floor saw strips of flesh fall around him that had been ripped from the shoulders of the fellow. The victim left the room, dragging after him strips of his skin and dripping blood. So, the master had chosen a young man for the sadistic forms of his lovemaking.

When the hair describes the master putting on his clothes and leaving the house, he gives an answer to the question the hero-voyeur had been asking. The master left for his heavenly dwelling, and the hair lying on the blood-covered floor was forgotten. But then, in a clap of thunder and a phosphorescent light, God (the master) reentered the room, and placed the hair back on His head. At this point the narration is spoken by God. When He had returned to heaven, His archangels had looked at Him with surprise and curiosity. They saw on His forehead drops of sperm and blood. When God felt the sperm and blood running down His cheeks and into His mouth, He was overcome with remorse. He was depraved and He acknowledged it.

The hair and the Master embrace like two friends meeting after a long separation. To the hair the Master confides His most intimate thoughts, especially the conviction that He is now inferior to the man He created out of a bit of sand and dust. God rehearses the laws of goodness and love He gave to humanity, of modesty and purity. How can men be expected to obey such laws when their Master refuses to be an example for them? He ends with the words: "my shame is as immense as eternity" (ma honte est immense comme l'éternité).

The hero, as spectator to this degrading scene, listens to the hair forgiving the Creator, and, as he makes his way through the labyrinthine streets of the city, he feels overcome with sadness at having such an enemy as an ancestor.

This scene of an avowed attack against the father-figure, in which the hero had witnessed the degradation of the father, as the sons of Noah had once witnessed their father's nakedness, parallels the scene of physical union with the mother, represented in the second canto, in the copulation of Maldoror with the female shark.

IV   Canto IV

Stanza 1. The opening stanza, far more than a mere introduction, is in itself almost a summary of the history of men. The "I" who speaks is Lautréamont, anxious to clarify for himself what has transpired on the earth to bring him to this moment. This moment he calls "war," not the war between man and man, but the more apocalyptic war between man and God.

Why is it, he questions at the beginning of the stanza, that when we touch another human being, we feel a sense of horror? This is a purely physical reaction, but there must be some explanation for this age-long habit of man turning against his fellowman. The stanza is a meditation on the strange character and the strange behavior of man.

The hardness of man is both his durability *(j'existe toujours comme le basalte)* and his cruelty. Even man's intelligence is a wall blocking him off from the world and from other men. Such a wall of stone is a symbol for the scorn which one man feels for the other. Lautréamont accepts this plight, now that he understands it, and says that this war against man will go on eternally: *que ma guerre contre l'homme s'éternise.* He is the one accepting this state of affairs more forthrightly than other men.

The stanza accumulates hard metal and stone to designate the eternity and the terrible force of this war: porphory, minerals extracted from the earth, iron, basalt. Two friends, each bent upon destroying the other, form the drama which the stanza elaborates. It summarizes what has gone on before in *Les Chants* and it announces what is to transpire now. The rule of the universe is not progress but destruction, or rather progress in methods of destruction.

Stanza 2. This is a striking and doubtless very important stanza where, after describing in a valley landscape two pillars that might be two baobabs or two towers or two pines, Lautréamont speaks directly to his reader. The four names for a phallic object and the tone of the writer as he speaks to the reader suggest analysis. The repression that is being discussed by the patient to his doctor is described by means of an image: a massive upright form.

Our lifelong habits engender irreparable stigmata. Lautréamont lists these habits as coming from or depending on: books, on relationships with other human beings, on the inherent characteristics of our temperament. In the light of the repetitiveness of our habits, it is difficult indeed to distinguish the comic from the melancholic because life is a comic drama or a dramatic comedy. This is the first conclusion in the stanza, and Lautréamont illustrates it in the form of a parody: Each of us is able to kill flies or rhinoceroses. Then he explains the method used to kill flies. Man's natural inclination to farce is one manifestation of his desire to reach truth.

Lautréamont mocks the philosopher who laughed when he saw a donkey eat a fig. At this point the writer confesses that he has never been able to laugh, and yet he was once witness of an event more hilarious than that of a donkey eating a fig. He saw a fig eat a donkey! The seriousness of farce is here related in a general sense to nature, to its monstrosities, and especially to the seeming unpredictableness of psychic nature in which long-held repressions may break out in ways that appear illogical.

The humor *(humour noir)* grows in this stanza and conducts the reader through passages that are quite purely surrealistic and where the language is an early form of Ionesco's style. Lautréamont decides not to tell his reader about ways by which to kill rhinoceroses. The phenomenon of laughter intrigues him. "Laugh," he advises, "but cry at the same time. If you find you are unable to cry through your eyes, cry through your mouth. If that's impossible, just urinate."

The ending of the stanza raises the question of the history of poetry. Lautréamont would seem to believe it has developed in a false way, by emphasizing the virtues of man, his sensibility, his sense of justice. Lautréamont adopts the other way: that of showing his vices and of divesting himself of all hypocrisy. This new ideal represents the meaning of the canto in which the attacks on man and the Creator will be made manifest . . .

In the way of a coda, Lautréamont returns in his last lines to the image of the two towers that were the first words of the stanza: *deux tours.* These two objects, symbols of the male sexual power, may be multiplied—and the product would be four. This multiplication is carried on symbolically by Maldoror's continuing on his way. Sexual fantasies, represented by the towers, are multiplied in the repressed life of the subconscious. One does not escape them by moving from place to place, with the ubiquity of Maldoror.

Stanza 3. The harassing quality of obsessions becomes clear in Stanza 3, where the opening word: *Une potence* (gallows) stands for the four phallic symbols of the preceding stanza: towers, pillars, pines, baobabs. In this opening word in which we see a stake or gallows, we also hear the word "potency," sexual potency of the male which becomes a theme in the explicit scene that follows.

A man is hanging by his hair from the *potence*. His hands are tied behind his back, his feet are free, and he is suffering such agony that he cries out he can last only one more hour in such a state. To Maldoror (or Lautréamont) he seems a stalagtite or a puppet or a ham strung up on a rope. As Maldoror steps out from his position of voyeur to help him, two women, highly intoxicated, come from the opposite direction. They carry instruments of torture: whips, rope, tar, brushes. There is such violence and frenzy in the eyes of both the older and the younger woman, that Maldoror cannot believe they belong to his race. If they are human, he thinks, they are the most hideous of all humans.

Their first words reveal their relationship with the victim: one is his wife and the other his mother. They cover the hanging body with tar and then lacerate it with whips. They beat the most sensitive parts they can reach: the face and the genitals. They continue thus until fatigue overcomes them—and again they withdraw. Maldoror comes to the rescue, cuts the hair of the victim after untieing his arms. The wretch then tells how his mother tried to seduce him and how his refusal angered his wife. Together the two women planned and carried out his torture.

This episode shows man, in his sexuality, being humiliated and rejected by women. There are strong echoes of Baudelaire *(Bénédiction* and *Voyage à Cythère)* throughout the scene where a man is hanging from a gallows and being tortured by his mother and wife because he refused to have sexual intercourse with his mother. The stanza also recalls the Crucifixion, with the suffering God hanging from the cross, and the women at the foot of the cross. As in *Voyage à Cythère,* the spectator (Maldoror) could also be looked upon as the figure being tortured.

Stanza 4. This stanza is in close relationship with the third, because here the body of man (after having been shown as hanging by its hair) is desecrated and metamorphosed, as in passages in Dante's *Inferno.* Those parts of the male body, associated with sexuality, penis, testicles, anus, buttocks, are inhabited and metamorphosed respectively by a viper, two small herons, a crab and two jellyfish.

All the familiar anxieties, associated with both adolescence and maturity in the hero's life, follow one another: the sense of evil that cannot be expelled, the will to martyrdom, the inexplicable persistence of hate, the desire to be immobilized and joined with the earth. Is this scene of immobilization and torture, the result of man (in the preceding stanza) having refused to commit incest? The immobilization would seem to be paternity *(O père infortuné)*, the last role of man that holds him securely bound until his death.

Stanza 5. The fear of castration is part of the obsessions in the third and fourth stanzas, but in the fifth it is predominant. In his mirror the hero sees himself as scalped and his head encircled by rapacious birds. The bald head is a classical symbol for the fear of castration. Without hair, the hero resembles a Redskin (the word *Peau Rouge* is used as it will be by Rimbaud in *Le Bateau ivre*). In order to put an end to the obsession or the nightmare, Maldoror smashes the mirror. He realizes that his eyes can bring on death.

This is, briefly put, the beginning and the end of a very difficult stanza. Throughout it, Maldoror is speaking to someone, and it would seem to be to himself, as reflected in the mirror, *sur le mur de ma chambre.* The *tu* he addresses is himself imprisoned in the mirror. This other self can live only there where he resembles a Redskin, because he has no hair. The passage is on the relationship between the two selves. The self in the mirror is more a disciple than a rival. He knows that if he tried to embrace the feet of the image, his arms would close around transparent vapor. The final act of smashing the mirror seems to come with the realization that he will never know, never understand his own image.

Stanza 6. Each of the remaining stanzas, 6, 7, 8, is related to the mature sexual life of man, or rather to the obsessions, the complexes that derive from sexuality. (Marcel Jean and Arpad Mezei would seem to be justified in this interpretation.)

The drama described in Stanza 6 is one of bestiality. Maldoror is a pig, living in filth, outside of humanity, and in such a condition that even the animals move off from him. In the scene, he is isolated on a cliff and calls his experience a metamorphosis. This experience of entering into the body of an animal, and living the life of an animal, represents a success in degrading the divine part of his human nature.

Stanza 7. The theme of bestiality and metamorphosis is continued in Stanza 7, one of the "story" stanzas in *Les Chants* and one of the most important in this canto. It is a plunge backward in time to an earlier existence when Maldoror's body possessed an amphibious nature.

It is the story of the amphibian *(amphibie),* man and animal in one body, a monster living in the water like a sea horse *(hippocampe),* in the air like a sea hawk *(orfraie),* under the sea like a mole *(taupe).* In his earliest memories he sees himself with a twin brother. But he was so handsome that his brother hated him and lied about him to their parents. Because of this betrayal, he was thrown into prison by his parents and tortured. There he experienced solitude of body and soul. From prison he made his escape to the seashore, and ultimately to the sea itself where he lived at peace with the fish. The amphibian is the monarch of the fish.

One after the other, Maldoror revives some of the archetypal dreams, dreams of escape into other forms and other existences that offset the immediate constraints of life. Anger and pride are the two basic sentiments or emotions that explain most of the immediate dramas of life, and that explain also the nightly regressions into the past where dreams reenact patterns of behavior that are often called deviations in man's conscious life. The first appearance of the amphibian, as in a dream sequence, is the breaking down of frontiers that normally separate the real from the surreal.

Stanza 8. In the final stanza, the fear of castration is more pronounced than ever. This time Maldoror evokes a more recent past, when he was fifteen years old, and was attracted to a blond youth of fourteen, called Falmer. The image of thick blond hair alternates with the image of a bald head, as bare as the shell of a turtle: *Eloignez donc cette tête sans chevelure, polie comme la carapace de la tortue.* The desire to attack Falmer sexually or mortally is confused in the evolving of this memory, with the fear of losing his virility.

After the passage in Stanza 7 on the brother's jealousy, which accounted for the amphibian's (Maldoror's) solitude, we come in Stanza 8 to what seems to be a more significant obsession, more deep-seated, more difficult to describe. The amphibian reminiscence does not evoke the idea of vengeance, but the blond youth

Falmer does become here the victim of revenge. The stanza begins with the words "night" *(chaque nuit)* and "memory" *(ma mémoire agonisante)*. Falmer rises up majestic and blond. Is it to denounce Maldoror?

In no other stanza of *Les Chants* does Lautréamont repeat so deliberately and so often the key phrases of the obsession or the drama which rises up from the past to torture his conscience: Falmer, his blond hair, his age. It would seem to be a sexual attack perpetrated by Maldoror on Falmer. Maldoror is stronger physically than Falmer. One day he seized Falmer by the hair, turned him around fast and hurled him against a tree trunk. Some of the boy's hair remained in his hand. The change of sperm to hair would be an easy transcription of an act which, when remembered, appears infamous. The repetition of the name, of the six letters of Falmer, is like the desired repetition of a sexual act, or of the repetition of a traumatic experience as it returns in dreams. "Each night." The words *chaque nuit* sound like a past act that continues to be re-enacted in the present, even as the young writer transcribes his meditation on paper. The collision of Falmer's body against the tree trunk transcribes the full force of the youth's orgasm.

V   Canto V

Throughout the fifth canto there is in evidence a stronger sense of age and maturity, and a growing need for abnormal behavior, for abnormal ways of satisfying desires. The obsessions are denser and more persistent.

Stanza 1. These obsessions are symbolized at the beginning of the canto by a flock of starlings *(étourneaux),* comparable to the cranes *(grues)* of Stanza 1 in Canto 1. The starlings reproduce the cyclical returns of obsessions whose blackness blots out everything else in the hero's world. Although the birds cut through the air swiftly, their flight is described as a whirlwind *(tourbillon).*

This image of a whirlwind is applicable to all of *Les Chants de Maldoror.* It reproduces the general movement of the entire work, the circling recurrent power of words, and the comparable return of obsessions, strong and persistent enough to efface aspects of conscious life. The center of the whirlwind is the initial traumatic experience, obscured by the gyrations that circumvent it.

But Lautréamont insists there is order behind the seeming disorder, and this leads him to a comparison between his writing and the whirlwind formed by the starlings and an attempt to ingratiate himself with the reader. He hopes that the seeming strangeness of his writing will not alienate the reader because he claims there is very little difference between his taste and the reader's. If the reader can open himself to poetry, he will understand and feel the bonds that join him with Lautréamont, and allow himself to be caught up in the whirlwind.

Stanza 2. Dominating the second stanza are two figures: a beetle *(un scarabée)* as large as a cow, and a man with the head of a pelican. The passage is difficult and deliberately confused. Maldoror himself sees imperfectly.

Before the figure of the man is seen as such, only his head is visible at the top of what seems to be a motionless column standing on the top of a mound. The beetle is moving toward the mound and rolling at the same time a ball of excrement. As Maldoror approaches the scene, still at some distance from it, he sees that the vertical object is a man with a bird's head in the place of his normally sized head. It is therefore a being with a double organism. Its mysteriousness is total for Maldoror, and rather than try to interpret it, he interrupts his thoughts with a Breton story of a wife's infidelity.

When the seafaring husband returned to Saint-Malo, he found his wife had just given birth to a baby, who could not be his own. He had her dress and forced her to walk with him on the ramparts of Saint-Malo at a moment when the north wind was blowing hard. As a result of this walk, the woman died during the night. Maldoror compares the relationship of that drama with the incomprehensible picture before him of the beetle and the man with a pelican's head.

The man speaks to the beetle and accuses him of rolling the ball which, rather than being excrement, is the mangled body of a woman. Another drama is taking place at the same time in the air: a momentous fight between a vulture *(le vautour des agneaux)* and an owl *(le grand-duc de Virginie)*. Everything in the scene is related to the implacable hostility man feels for man. The woman, whose crushed body is being rolled like a ball, was a magician who had given one man a pelican's head and transformed his brother into a beetle. These are four existences: pelican, beetle, owl and vulture, that can now be scratched off from the book of life. Everything is antithetical: the pelican, erect and phallic-like; the beetle, anal in its excremental preoccupation; the vulture, a day bird; the owl, a night bird.

Stanza 3. Sleeplessness is a theme in Stanza 3 where the recurring obsessions each night are related to birth and death for Maldoror. He stands erect at his window throughout the night and looks out at the stars. Dawn finds him in this position. To the sleeper his body is a corpse, and the sheets of his bed a shroud. Maldoror's endless meditation on himself *(ma subjectivité)* and on the Creator is too much for his mind to bear.

Maldoror envies those who sleep peacefully. He fears sleep because of its revelations, and does everything he can to avoid falling asleep. The dreams of sleep would make him into more than he is, into a plurality of beings. As long as he exists, he is no one else. *Si j'existe, je ne suis pas un autre.* (An interesting contradiction of what Rimbaud says: *Je est un autre.*) The sinking into sleep for Maldoror would be comparable to sinking into eternity and hearing its uproar, as one can hear the sound of the sea at a distance. Sleep would mean the blotting out of the familiar room where he lives. It is important that his eyes never close.

Stanza 4. Maldoror's conscience, in Stanza 4, appears in various forms: as a python with its ever-moving coils, a boa, a basilisk. His sense of remorse is confused with murmurings and plottings. When he assigns to the boa a primitive majesty *(ta sauvage majesté),* he would seem to be confusing or identifying his conscience with the Creator. The stanza is an apostrophe addressed to his conscience-Creator whose leading aberration is the failure to recognize Maldoror. The Creator in his reign of domination and injustice has gone through endless metamorphoses in his efforts to terrify. Maldoror persists in saying that the day of his triumph is not far off. But there is always the hallucinating sense of pity for the Creator, for his conscience whom he condemned to a life of wandering and solitude. As he, Maldoror, grows in power and affluence, his Creator will decline in poverty and impotence.

Stanza 5. The apostrophe of Stanza 5 is addressed this time to pederasts *(O pédérastes incompréhensibles),* and Lautréamont describes the prostitution of those men who offer themselves to the first comer. As always, Maldoror becomes one of those he apostrophizes, as if, in order to fulfill his hero's destiny, he must know all the aberrations of mankind. The Creator engages also in this office, and, in the last line of the stanza, opens his door to a pederast. (Here, as in contemporary French literature and speech, the word "pederast" is used inaccurately in the place of the more accurate word "homosexual.")

The combined tones of derision and clinical observation make the stanza difficult to decipher in terms of Maldoror's attitude toward homosexuality. Such words in the stanza as "degradation," "shame," "punishment," have a biblical resonance of accusation. But there is also a Greek-Platonic theorizing in the passage where the homosexual is praised and revered for his superior moral beauty. However, in such passages he is apostrophized as feminine. The act of sodomy is described in terms of brutality and violence. The role of the sodomist is one more metamorphosis of Maldoror, and in this role he likes neither woman nor hermaphrodite. He complains that the lovemaking has gone on so long and so intensely that he has lost all desire for it and all potency.

Maldoror, aggressively homosexual in his attacks on adolescents, reveals the attraction he feels for schools and factories, and for the memories of his crimes. He was never caught by the agents of the law, although on one occasion he even murdered his sexual partner and disposed of the body in an abandoned well. He proudly speaks of the fear he should inspire in the young and their sinister attraction to the spectacle of his aroused penis. Throughout the world, South America, Egypt, many have been enticed by the smell of the preseminal drops on his organ. The fantasy-image grows to spectacular dimensions as Maldoror gloats over the sexual attraction of his body. He hides from those who want to make love to him, in order to torment them and arouse them all the more. The passage is reminiscent of the scene in *Genesis* where the men of Sodom approach the house of Lot and call out for the two angels to be released to them. The sexual fantasy of Maldoror is like a talisman given to him by God.

Stanza 6. As is frequent in Lautréamont's art, a sudden change of scene occurs with Stanza 6, and we see a funeral procession for a ten-year-old boy. This is the occasion for a meditation on the death-instinct, or the death-wish, which is closely allied with a feeling of impotence. Maldoror watches the burial, and then gallops away. The apocalyptic horse returns frequently in the work. This time he is described as a twisting cyclone *(un cyclone giratoire).* Lautréamont ends the stanza by having the priest state his conviction that the dead boy is in reality living and that the strange figure on horseback is dead.

The ten-year-old boy disappeared from the earth as mysteriously and easily as an ordinary fly *(mouche)* or a dragonfly *(libellule).* This comparison, and others in the stanza, bring out the theme of the oneness of being in the world, the amphibian quality of man, and the human quality of amphibians. The description of the funeral is not as tragic as it is ironic. It leads to digressions on priests and families, on the exile of a child from his family. Whatever we observe, as Maldoror does in watching the funeral procession, we try instinctively to find resemblances and differences that both relate us to and separate us from the world.

A beautiful passage on the flight of the kite *(le milan)* high in the air, far above the opened casket of the dead boy, leads to such a query on the part of Maldoror. What is the relationship between the bird and the boy? There is a majestic calm in the wings of the bird and on the face of the boy. We often forget to admire the beauty of things we habitually see every day. The illustration to this lesson is in the priest who, as he prays over the grave of the boy, sees the galloping figure of Maldoror as the figure of Death.

Stanza 7. The betrayal of friendship is a persistent theme in *Les Chants de Maldoror,* and in the final stanza of Canto V, it is more deliberately developed than elsewhere.

Maldoror's distrust of friendship, or his incapacity for friendship, goes very far in explaining his solitude. At the beginning of the stanza, as a prelude, is the episode of the old spider *(une vieille araignée)* that emerges from a hole in the floor to suck Maldoror's blood every night when he is asleep. The spider is the symbol of friendship because from its belly emerge the two friends: Elsseneur and Réginald. (The English names recall the Gothic tales that are

among the literary sources of *Les Chants*.) The suffering inflicted
on Maldoror by his friends is implicit in the story of the attack
made on Réginald when his right wrist is severed from his body.
The Lord, who is never absent for very long from the narration,
has ordered the metamorphosis of the two friends into the spider
destined to haunt Maldoror's bed and symbolize the failure of
friendship.

Maldoror's nightly fear of falling asleep, and thus leaving himself vulnerable to the spider, is described in detail. How can he un-
cover the meaning of the nightmare and recover from his loss of
blood? In similar detail, the appearance and the approach of the
spider are described. Then Lautréamont seems to intervene and
speaks directly to Maldoror and tells him that soon he will understand the nightly happening and the power of Elsseneur's face on his
imagination. And he will understand also the proud stance of
Réginald. . . . One is led finally to believe that all of this comes from
an episode of Maldoror's youth which he is trying to recall and
comprehend. He may also be afraid of comprehending it.

At this point, the clear speech of Lautréamont stops and the allegory begins when we see the boys Elsseneur and Réginald emerge
from the spider's belly and stand beside Maldoror's bed, as guardians
of his sleep. At first Réginald was loved by Maldoror, but he soon
suffered from the brusqueness of Maldoror's behavior. Once they
swam off, Réginald began losing his strength. There were traces of
his blood in the water. When Réginald called out for help, Maldoror continued to swim and uttered a sensuous cry *(un cri de
volupté)*. The swimming in the sea continued for an hour during
which time one boy continued to lose his strength and the other
grew in strength. Just before Réginald would have succumbed,
some fishermen pulled him aboard their boat. They saw that a wound
in the boy's right side must have been caused by a sharp knife. . . .
As Réginald stood by the bedside of Maldoror, he thought of that
betrayal and wept.

Then begins the second story, that of Elsseneur. When Elsseneur
first felt love for Maldoror, it seemed to him like a supernatural
experience, and he wondered whether Maldoror had fallen to earth
from some planet. In this passage, Elsseneur tells his own story,
and describes the walks he and Maldoror used to take through
the woods. He remembers that a wild boar *(un sanglier)* wept when

he saw the two boys together. When they passed fortifications, they avoided the sentinels.

At the entrance to a forest, Maldoror stopped before a birch tree *(un bouleau)* and ordered Elsseneur to prepare to die. He threw the boy to the ground and held him there with one knee on his chest. Maldoror had to work fast because a herd of oxen was approaching and the herder might bring help. He drew a knife from his belt and cut off Elsseneur's right wrist. The hand, neatly severed, fell to the ground. Maldoror took flight.

Like an epic narrative or a legend, the story continues. The herder helped cure Elsseneur who then became a soldier, and a feared soldier because of the power of his artificial iron hand. In the course of a fierce battle, an equally powerful knight on the adversary's side was disputing the victory with Elsseneur. The two armies stopped fighting to watch the two individual champions. They fought on without one winning. When they stopped to rest, they raised their visors. Elsseneur recognized Réginald. Both fellows had taken on the same career because of their love for Maldoror.

The despair and the sadness in their lives were the same. Their frustrated love for Maldoror joined them in deep friendship. An archangel from Heaven ordered them to change into one spider that each night would suck blood from the neck of Maldoror. For ten years this nightly ritual was carried out. The trial now came to an end. Maldoror woke up and saw two celestial forms, closely embraced, disappear into the air. He realized that the nightly experience was over.

He drank from a crystal pitcher and opened the blinds of the window. He waited for the morning light which would bring relief to his tormented heart. But this final word "relief" *(soulagement)* appears with the adjective "derisive" *(dérisoire)*. The cure is only temporary. The obsession we have been reading in Stanza 7 has been interrupted momentarily. The fifth canto is not the end of the work. The sixth will resume the obsession, but in a different form.

VI   Canto VI

Stanza 1. Throughout the final canto, the author intervenes more constantly than heretofore, in direct speech to the reader, to explain and justify the work. The opening stanza is this kind of communication in which *Les Chants de Maldoror* is defined as an insult to man, to the Creator, and to Lautréamont! The purpose of the writing is to attack man and his Creator. The author has no intention of retracting his words. He announces a story of thirty pages which will enable the reader to comprehend better Lautréamont's position of renegade and the diabolical influences on him: *la préface du renégat, à la figure fuligineuse.*

The passage is the author speaking about technical matters in his writing. His three characters: man, the Creator and himself he calls *les ficelles du roman,* the "strings" or the devices of the story, as if the characters were puppets controlled by strings. But these characters come so close to the face of the reader that he sees their bodies, their physiological functions, their limitless energy. The first five stories (or cantos) were necessary, but they were merely the frontispiece, the synthetic part of the work that should have told the reader that Lautréamont's main purpose is to attack man and the Creator who made him. For the moment, and forever, there is no need for the reader to know any more. Then Lautréamont establishes the omniscience of himself the writer and the servility or ingenuousness of the reader who waits patiently for the outcome of the story, but who will never fully comprehend it.

In pedagogic fashion, and using such terms as "thesis" and "development," Lautréamont announces that his intention is now to proceed to the analytical part of his work. His argumentation will resemble a theorem. When he accuses humanity, it should not be forgotten that he is a member of humanity. The analysis, then, is the short novel of thirty pages, about to begin. The "novel" *(roman)* is the definitive formula for Lautréamont. What has preceded it, in the form of a preface, is hybrid. The "novel" is pure, unique, and hence, incomprehensible.

Stanza 2. With the second stanza, the genre of the work is acknowledged in the behavior of the hero. Maldoror cannot be siezed. He changes his form constantly. He is ubiquitous. Agents, spies, disguises characterize the world of *notre héros.* He can turn into a cricket in the Paris sewers. One day he is in Madrid, the next day in Saint Petersburg, and the day after that he is in Peking. He is the type of hero-adventurer who has appeared in every age. He is the magician of the medieval tale, the sadist of the Gothic tale, Robin Hood, James Bond, one of the witches in Sade's *Juliette,*

Fantômas, Batman, Superman, Jesse James. The list is endless, because man's drama of liberation is endless, and his hope of transcending laws, both physical and moral, and his determination to change his human fate are also endless.

At the beginning of the passage, Maldoror speaks of the perverse instinct of destructiveness that is in him, and he calls it by the curious and revelatory term "the minotaur of his perverse instincts *(le minotaure de ses instincts pervers).* He therefore approaches his victims, "human agglomerations," as if he were a beast of prey. He compares himself on the one hand to a mythological monster, and on the other hand he is the contemporary genius, clever in disguises, who eludes spies and agents. Ubiquitous in terms of space, Maldoror also has the memory of all forms of conquests and carnage throughout history.

At the end of the stanza, he picks up his pen and concludes with a mysterious sentence, the first of a series of final sentences that end each of the chapters. Maldoror wonders how "the Pont du Carrousel could remain indifferent when it heard the screams coming from the bag." These are the words that personify the inanimate object of a bridge and that would seem to announce a violent melodramatic story.

Stanza 3 (divided into eight chapters)
I.   The story then begins. It will occupy eight chapters and bring to a conclusion *Les Chants de Maldoror*. It is the story of Mervyn and Maldoror, the story of a spiritual seduction and a physical assassination, which is probably the reversal of what Lautréamont had in mind: a physical seduction and a spiritual assassination.

There is considerable geographical precision in the Paris that is evoked in this story. It begins on the rue Vivienne, in the vicinity of the Bibliothèque Nationale and the Bourse. Night is falling. Shutters are being closed. Solitude and darkness are settling over the city. Everyone is anxious to leave this part of the city and reach home. What has happened to the street? Where are the gas lamps and the prostitutes? An owl flying over the Madeleine Church cries out: "A disaster is coming." *(Un malheur se prépare.)* Against this setting, at the point of intersection between the rue Colbert and the rue Vivienne, appears the silhouette of a man or of one who would be taken as a mature person from a distance.

It is a sixteen-year-old boy, Mervyn, who, having taken a fencing lesson, is on his way home. His beauty is such that language is inadequate to describe it, but the shock that his beauty creates is put into a sentence that was destined to attract the Surrealists and André Breton especially. A meeting with Mervyn is comparable to the encounter on a dissecting table of a sewing machine and an umbrella: *comme la rencontre fortuite sur une table de dissection d'une machine à coudre et d'un parapluie!*

Mervyn is being followed by Maldoror. The boy feels the presence of some malefic influence. The infernal machine is at work. At times Maldoror comes close to Mervyn in order to impress upon himself the features of the boy. And at other times he withdraws as if undecided about what he is doing or should do. Mervyn walks faster with a growing dread that something is wrong. It would be easy to escape from the threatening presence near him, but he is ignorant of the danger. Mervyn is no prophet. He comes to the big boulevards, and crosses the boulevard Poissonnière and the boulevard Bonne-Nouvelle. He enters the rue du Faubourg-Saint-Denis, and stops before a high doorway.

This brief introductory chapter ends with an allusion to an iron ring hidden under a stone by the hand of a maniac. When Maldoror (or Lautréamont) thinks of such an object, he shudders. The iron ring is comparable to the Pont du Carrousel in the final sentence of the preceding passage.

II. The boy pulls the copper bell and the large door opens. He crosses the courtyard and climbs the eight steps of the porch. Two statues, placed like guards at the inner door, do not bar his entrance into the aristocratic villa.

Maldoror, for the pursuit of evil, has given up everything (mother, father, God, love, ideals), and lives mysteriously alone. He does not follow Mervyn into the house, but is able to watch the boy's movements inside his family's villa. Mervyn has everything: the love of his parents, a beautiful home, fashionable clothes. This particular evening the boy appears changed, listless, inattentive. The parents fear a spell is on him. The father speaks of tracking down the man who has cast the spell, and of killing him.

Mervyn's mother is English. She asks permission of her husband to get a bottle of the essence of turpentine which may help dispel the disturbance in her son. The scene is one of rigid court etiquette.

A servant hands the bottle to the mother, who hands it to the father. An Indian silk scarf is dipped in the liquid and wound around Mervyn's head. He seems to revive, and yet he half understands there is an evil presence nearby. He half remembers the walk home along the boulevards. He tries to reassure his parents and calls for his small brothers. But again he falls into a state of lethargy. A physician is called who states, on examining Mervyn, that the crisis is passed and that all will be well in the morning.

Maldoror, in a way that is never made clear, has followed all the activity. He has learned the plan of the house and the location of Mervyn's room. He leaves the estate by climbing over the iron fence. It was not his intention to seize the boy at that time.

The chapter ends with Maldoror speaking to his reader and telling him to go to the swan lake where he will see a black swan bearing an anvil *(enclume)* with the body of a crab. The other swans are justifiably suspicious of the intruder. Here the *enclume* is the hard metal which joins, like a further emblem, the Carrousel Bridge and the iron ring.

III.   Late that night, in his room, Mervyn receives a strange letter that Maldoror had sent through the mail. He knows that as an obedient son he should show it to his father. But he places the letter on some richly bound books, and in an effort to recover from the emotion he feels, he plays the piano. No sounds come forth from the instrument. He identifies this mystery with the letter, and, his curiosity stronger than his fear, he opens it and reads. The letter is a call to embrace love and adventure. Maldoror calls for a five o'clock morning rendezvous in two days on the Pont du Carrousel. The letter speaks of exotic travels the two will take, the protection that Maldoror will offer Mervyn, and the assurance of his love. There is a warning not to show the letter to anyone.

With the reading of this letter (all the melodramatic effects are called into use in this episode), Mervyn's bewitchment deepens. His mind opens to new limitless horizons. For the first time, he begins to see defects in his mother and father and brothers. During school the next day, his teachers see a marked change in him. Each one of them fears himself intellectually unable to compete with Mervyn.

That evening the scene at home is elaborately described: the rich dinner, the wines, the Bohemian glasses on the table. But Mervyn appears like a somnambulist. The father, once a commander *(un commodore)* decides to read a story to the family in order to distract his oldest son. It is a story of voyages, and because of that, Mervyn pays attention at the beginning. But soon he is unable to follow the reading.

The father then urges his wife to read another kind of story. At first her voice sounds melodious to Mervyn, but he interrupts the reading and retires to his room. Everything participates in the spell that Maldoror has cast: a dog howling, the wind blowing through a window crack and twisting the flame in a lamp. The mother, the father, and even the young sons are affected.

Once in his room, Mervyn writes a long letter in answer to the letter he had carried on his person all that day. This letter of Mervyn occupies a large part of the chapter. At the beginning, he confesses his worry whether he should indeed answer at all. But he argues with himself that it would be impolite not to answer a stranger who is interested in him. He imagines that Maldoror is older than he is because Maldoror addresses him as "young man" *(jeune homme)*. But he is uncertain about Maldoror's age. His uncertainty comes from the difference between the cold syllogistic reasoning in the letter and the fervor that he finds in it.

Although he states that he cannot leave on the distant voyage without permission from his parents, he does agree to the early morning rendezvous, and says that he will climb over the park wall and that no one will see him leave. The letter, as it continues, grows in strangeness and boldness, as if Mervyn has already undergone the indoctrination of Maldoror, or as if all the instincts of revolt and licentiousness had risen up in the adolescent. He knows the art of seduction without ever having been seduced or without ever having seduced.

Frankly and clearly he writes. He would do anything for Maldoror because he is overcome by the inexplicable attachment the stranger has shown for him. He implores his friend not to fail to be present on the Pont du Carrousel at the appointed hour. He wants to touch him with his hand, although he has heretofore refrained from any bodily contact with anyone. Such a sentence as this would indicate that Mervyn understands he is embarking upon an experience of serious intimacy.

He leaves his letter unsigned and thus imitates Maldoror. He is prepared to be surprised at nothing, and only wonders how Maldoror had found out about him, how he had known about the solemn-looking home in which he lives and the boredom of his life there. The final lines of the letter are those of a new love. He feels already attached to Maldoror and goes down on his knees before him as he embraces his unknown liberator.

After posting the letter, Mervyn feels guilt for having written it and returns to his room where there is no guardian angel at his bed. This time the final lines of the chapter contain more than one hard object as a mysterious emblem terminating and perhaps representing the episode that has just been read. A beam *(une poutre)*, a bullet *(une balle),* and fourteen daggers *(quatorze poignards)* seem to involve a series of legends of violence and struggle. Are these cabalistic, hieroglyphic signs? Or are they examples of automatic writing? They seem to have no relationship with the story.

IV.   The narrative itself is at this point interrupted by two brief passages that are related to Mervyn's fate, but only in a general sense.

Maldoror (or Lautréamont) speaks from beginning to end of Chapter IV. He notices that he has only one eye in the middle of his forehead. Like Cyclops, he is a monster and reviews a partial list of his acts of monstrosity. He represents a duality which would seem to be his beauty and his demonic powers.

His beauty is unusual and associated with vice. He compares it to the strange formation of the penis, especially in the distance between the canal of the urethra and the glans of the penis. This moment of self-examination in a mirror convinces him there is no longer any need for lying because he is not envious of the Creator. His power now allows him to challenge God who is permitting him to descend the river of his destiny. The words he uses are almost identical to those used by Rimbaud in the first line of *Le Bateau ivre:*

Rimbaud: *Comme je descendais des Fleuves impassibles*
Lautréamont: *le Créateur me laisse descendre le fleuve de ma destinée.*

Rimbaud's boat descend the river to encounter various experiences of violence and beauty. Mervyn's river leads him through a series of "glorious crimes" *(crimes glorieux).*

Maldoror bids farewell to God, his enemy whom he calls "illustrious warrior," and tells him they will soon meet again in order to dispute their power over the next victim—Mervyn. Again, the ending of the passage is unrelated to the rest, and emphasizes material objects: "candelabrum" *(candélabre)*, a "large crab" *(le crabe tourteau)*.

V.   The precise naming of Paris typography continues in this chapter. The first scene is at the Palais Royal, on a bench near a pond in the garden. A fellow had come there from the rue de Rivoli. His hair is messed up, his clothes are rags, and he has just dug up some earth and tried to eat it. He puts his head on the bench and his feet in the air as if he were a tight-rope walker. But he soon falls back against the bench.

Maldoror, standing in a position where he can see everything, has been watching the gymnastics of the fellow who is obviously deranged. He comes over to help him and places him in a normal position. The man's madness is intermittent and he is able to answer the questions asked by Maldoror.

The narration of his miserable life occupies a large part of the chapter. It is a scene worthy of Diderot and *la comédie larmoyante:* a drunken father, three sisters, the brother, a pet canary loved by all the family except the father. In a drunken rage, the father crushes the canary cage, and soon the bird dies. The three sisters *(les trois marguerite)* crawl into the dog's kennel and die there. This episode brings on the brother's madness. He lives by begging for charity.

A bandit (obviously Maldoror) pretends compassion, takes care of him, takes him home to an elegant apartment, and crowns him "king of wisdom" *(roi des intelligences)*. A change takes place in the wretched fellow. He falls on his knees before his benefactor. He is the crowned fool, ready to serve in every way his master, who is Maldoror, and who is described as having bronze lips *(l'homme aux lèvres de bronze.)*

The reason for the long narrative becomes clear with the naming of the new servant: Aghone. It is he who will stand up under every trial, who is sufficiently naïve to obey every order. The chance encounter in the Palais Royal garden is favorable to Maldoror. He has found an accomplice who cannot distinguish good from evil. Maldoror needed Aghone.

VI.   The main narrative concerning Mervyn is now resumed, and auspiciously, with the intervention of the Almighty who sends down to the earth one of his archangels to save the adolescent from certain death. Lautréamont again takes his reader into his confidence with the remarks that he must not move too fast, that any melodramatic effect or trick *(truc)*, will have to come in its own time.

In order not to be recognized, the archangel has taken the form of a turtle crab: *un crabe tourteau,* as large as a vicuna *(vigogne).* It is first seen resting on a reef in the ocean and waiting for the ebbing of the tide in order to reach the shore. It will be remembered that the *crabe tourteau* was one of the emblematic signs at the end of Chapter IV.

The family scene of Chapter V was reminiscent of sentimental popular novels of the eighteenth and nineteenth centuries. Lautréamont's leading theme of Maldoror's struggle against God and against the emissaries of God becomes again central in the sixth chapter and continues to the end of the work.

From this point on until the end, during which the action mounts to monstrous proportions, the lips of Maldoror are often described and always with a different color: *bronze, jaspe, saphir, soufre.* The metallic hardness of his lips seems to symbolize his skill of demon.

As the archangel-crab remains on his rock, and as Maldoror hides in a bend of the shore, they engage upon a kind of debate in which the crab speaks three times and Maldoror twice. The first speech of the crab is said to himself. He acknowledges that his mission is difficult, that he is in a limited substance, and that little is known about his adversary. But choirs of angels in heaven have said that Maldoror is more to be feared than Satan himself.

In like manner, Maldoror's first speech is directed to himself. He estimates the lack of experience of the crab. He argues to himself that this disguised angel has been sent by the Almighty who fears to come himself. The crab's seraphic origin is revealed in his wandering indecisive eyes. When the crab finally sees Maldoror, he speaks directly to him asking him to surrender. Then God's enemy will be put in chains so that his fingers will clasp no new daggers. A surrender will be a first step toward repentance.

Maldoror finds this apostrophe comical and laughs outright. In fact, he almost chokes over his laughter. He derides God who, unwilling to come himself, sends snails and crawfish in his place. He encourages the crab to come down from his fortress and swim to the shore, so that the conditions for some kind of surrender *(reddition)* may be drawn up.

These words sounded so encouraging to the crab that his head slightly emerged from his shell and he spoke fervently, calling upon Maldoror to repent and take his place once again among the angels. He likens Maldoror to Lucifer who once occupied the first place in the angelic hosts. He pleads with Maldoror to make an enduring peace with his master.

Maldoror has been watching his chance for a dark stratagem. By the end of the crab's speech, his body has emerged totally from the opening of the shell. He is fully exposed on the reef, self-assured, like a priest certain of recovering a lost sheep. He was about to swim in the direction of Maldoror. But at that moment, the sapphire-lipped man threw a stick *(un bâton)* with such a force that it struck the crab's head. It fell into the water mortally wounded. Like a piece of wreckage, the crab floated to the shore where the incoming tide deposited it. Maldoror embraced his "two friends": the homicidal stick and the body of the crab. He is pleased with himself for having retained his physical skill.

Feeling he must hide the body, he puts it, with an anvil, on his back. The two words *enclume* and *crabe tourteau* were at the emblematic ending of Chapter II, and here their function is made clear. Maldoror goes to a large lake whose banks are covered with tall rushes. He intends to crush the body into powder by means of the heavy anvil.

On arriving at the lake, he sees it inhabited by swans. He changes himself into a black swan and swims three times among the white birds. Instinctively these native swans keep away from Maldoror, who remains in the center of the lake. As a bird, Maldoror stays isolated from other birds. Even as a man, he remains isolated from other men. This is the prelude to the unbelievable event of the Place Vendôme.

VII. Lautréamont is trying to build up suspense in his story in the manner of a popular novelist.

Maldoror, on reading Mervyn's letter, understands the intellectual torment the boy went through. Mervyn had accepted and, curiously because of his inexperience, understood all the equivocal connotations of the rendezvous. He left his home at the correct time, followed the boulevard Sébastopol to the fountain of Saint Michel. As he walked along the quai Malaquais, he saw a man carrying a sack walking parallel to him along the quai du Louvre. This unknown figure seemed to be watching him carefully.

The morning mist had risen. From both ends, the two walkers began crossing the Pont du Carrousel. They recognized one another. If there had been an onlooker, he would have been moved by the noble sentiments that seemed to inhabit these two beings as they approached one another. Mervyn was weeping because he believed he was meeting a man who would sustain him through all future adversities.

Maldoror said nothing. He unfolded the sack he was carrying, opened it, and seizing Mervyn by the head, forced the entire body of the boy into the sack. He tied the opening with a handkerchief. When Mervyn began screaming, Maldoror struck the bag, as if it were full of laundry, against the parapet of the bridge. The boy, realizing his bones were being broken, stopped his cries.

Lautréamont enjoys the scene he is describing. He calls it unique and says that no novelist will ever rediscover it.

A butcher passed at that moment with his cart of meat. Maldoror gives him the bag and says it contains a dog suffering from mange *(la gale)* that must be slaughtered. The butcher tells three of his colleagues that the dog in the bag must be killed. Each takes a hammer to perform the act, but there is such commotion in the bag that one of the butchers hesitates and begins wondering if it is really a dog that is howling and trying to escape. The butchers argue briefly until one opens the bag and pulls out the almost stifled body of Mervyn. He faints on seeing the light of day. The butchers take to their heels in fright. Mervyn, with deep forebodings, returns home and locks himself in his room.

Lautréamont then tells his readers that the dénouement of the story is coming fast. There is no need to prolong or inflate it. It is better to speak briefly and then be silent.

VIII.   This is the end of the story when Aghone resumes his role. At the beginning, Lautréamont continues his discussion with the reader. He promises again to be brief and calls himself the hypnotizer of the reader.

The crab came back to life. It pulled out of a hole the tail of a fish, gave it the two wings of an albatross which permitted the tail to fly off. It flew in the direction of the renegade (God) in order to betray Maldoror, but Maldoror guessed the intention and shot a poisoned arrow into the fish's tail. It died before reaching the earth.

Then an ancient beam *(une poutre)* in the roof of a castle rose up and cried for vengeance. But the Almighty, in the form of a rhinoceros, assured it that the death of the fish's tail was deserved. The beam quieted down, resumed its horizontal place, and told the spiders to continue spinning their webs. When Maldoror *(l'homme aux lèvres de soufre)* learns this weakness of his ally *(la poutre),* he orders Aghone to burn the beam and reduce it to ashes. Aghone carries out the order.

Maldoror announces that the moment has finally come, and gives Aghone a package of rope. He assured himself then that the fourteen daggers *(poignards)* obediently waited for orders. The signs of death accumulate when Aghone speaks of seeing a cock split in two with its beak a candelabrum and cry out: "There is little distance between the rue de la Paix and the place du Panthéon."

From this point on to the end, the narrative is fast moving, dense, cinematographic with parts of scenes superimposed one on the other. It is a surrealist phantasmagoria when the crab appears on a spirited horse rushing toward the reef in the ocean which had witnessed the hurling of the stick and which had been the shelter for its descent to earth. Already a caravan of pilgrims was on its way to visit that site which a celebrated death had consecrated. The crab did not reach the spot in time to ask help and thus prevent the scene that was already unfolding.

The buildup, in its melodramatic-surrealistic style, is now complete for the scene to begin. Mervyn appears. He is unrecognizable. His hands are tied behind his back, and he walks as if on his way to the gallows. Yet he is without guilt of any kind. At the Place Vendôme, a man who is leaning on the balustrade of the column, fifty meters above the ground, unrolls a cable and throws it into the air. It lands a few feet from Aghone who immediately ties the end of the cable to Mervyn's feet.

The epic *merveilleux* importance of the moment is underscored by the appearance of the rhinoceros on the rue Castiglione. He is shot at by a man who is armed with a revolver. The mother and father of Mervyn try, but unsuccessfully, to protect the rhinoceros. The bullet pierces his body, but the animal, since part of him is divine, does not die.

The scene shifts to the man at the top of the column who pulls the cable and begins swinging Mervyn back and forth. Mervyn is now hanging by his feet, his head pointed down. The movement of the swinging body is like a sling as it circles the bronze obelisk. In its air circumference, the body is kept equidistant from the column. When the body has gathered considerable speed, the man holding the cable releases it. Mervyn, like a comet with its flaming tail speeding after it, flies through the air in the direction of the left bank, and strikes against the dome of the Pantheon. The cord wraps around the boy's body. And today, if you look carefully, you will see a dried skeleton at the top of the cupola. Students in the Latin Quarter when they fear such a death as Mervyn's, often say a prayer as they look up at the dome.

The work ends thus, histrionically, melodramatically, surrealistically, in the realization of a death wish, in a scene so contrived that everything disappears. Even the skeleton at the top of the Pantheon is only imperfectly visible. Such a nightmarish scene was necessary for Maldoror to free himself from his drive to rival God. It represents the kind of action that is both traumatic and therapeutic. By violence one rids oneself of violence. Having lived through such a scene, Maldoror could never live again in the way that had been the subject matter of the six *chants*.

We can easily imagine a cure taking place in Maldoror after the fulgurant sacrificial death scene of Mervyn. Man cannot live for long in a spirit of revolt without its killing him. The writer Lautréamont is ready for *Poésies,* a work that seems to have no connection with *Les Chants.* After mesmerizing his reader (he used the term *crétiniser le lecteur*), he will talk with him in a different tone, with different preoccupations. In its turn, *Poésies* will be the prelude to the real death of Isidore Ducasse. The writings and the life of Lautréamont are the passage from defiance to recovery and to death.

A garland of everlasting flowers *(immortelles)* is referred to twice on the last page of the sixth *chant.* It seems to be twined around the cable that hurls Mervyn into space and to his death. The horror of the scene is thus diminished and explained by the very resonance of the word *immortelle.* The death-bearing cable is metamorphosed into a symbol of eternity at the very moment when an intricately conceived scene to demonstrate a violent death was being enacted.

CHAPTER 4

Poésies

I Poésies I

IN an explanatory letter, Lautréamont had said he intended to take to task the best poems of Lamartine, Hugo, Musset, Byron and Baudelaire, and rewrite them in the light of hope. (Letter to Verbroeckhoven, 21 February 1870.) Either this work was never done, or the two pamphlets of *Poésies,* published in April and June, 1870, were the work, at least in part. According to another hypothesis, the two *Poésies* may have been intended to serve as a preface to the new work. *Poésies* is certainly a criticism of the Romantic poetry of doubt and despair. When André Breton published the work in the second issue of *Littérature* (April, 1919), he was aware that there was no relationship between *Les Chants de Maldoror* and *Poésies.* "They are not comparable," he wrote, "but *Poésies* is not inferior to *Les Chants.*"

On the dedication page, Lautréamont calls the new writing *prosaïques morceaux.* It has little to do with the subconscious, which was, after all, the major theme of *Les Chants.* It is a more classical, more literal-minded work that would seem to be a kind of program or manifesto for new literature.

Twelve names are listed in the dedication, as well as a general dedication to "friends past, present and future." The first and the last names are probably the most important: Georges Dazet, Ducasse's closet friend at the *lycée* of Tarbes, who at his death in 1920, was known as a militant Socialist, and Hinstin, who was Ducasse's teacher at the *lycée of Pau.*

The epigraph of *Poésies,* a few lines long, is a clearly stated moralistic sentence in which Lautréamont claims he is replacing melancholy by courage, doubt by certainty, despair by hope, evil by God, skepticism by faith, sophistry by clear thinking, and pride by modesty.

The opening maxim is a logical continuation of the epigraph. Lautréamont calls the poetic lamentation of his century sophistry.

This is the typical attack of the young writer against his literary heritage, against all those successful figures in his immediate past who now seem false to him. This kind of attack is in Rimbaud's early letters, especially those of May 13 and 15, 1871. It is the younger writer's valiant effort to speak out with his own voice.

The second sentence is the new metaphysical position of Lautréamont in which he accepts the "first principles" and places them apart from any possible discussion: God is to be revered. . . . The season of *Les Chants de Maldoror* is passed. In the Romantic age, the writer was looked upon as ill, and his reader as a sympathetic guardian. That attitude is no longer held. The poet should be consoler and guardian of humanity. His "illness" is in reality his perceptive understanding and his strength. Since Lautréamont will not leave memoirs of his life, he has ceased being the Romantic. The poetry of Young *(Nights),* so universally admired by the French Romantic writers, is condemned by Lautréamont in his new assessment.

In a lengthy Rabelaisian-like listing, which begins: *Les perturbations, les anxiétés, les dépravations,* Lautréamont rehearses all the Romantic themes and superstitiions. The enumeration is condemnation, but it is totally Romantic in its choice of nouns and epithets. At the end, Lautréamont specifically denounces the prefaces of Hugo *(Cromwell),* Gautier *(Mlle de Maupin),* and Dumas fils (prefaces to his plays).

The condemnation continues with pointed references to Scott, Cooper, Balzac, Alexander Dumas, and seems to be based on a belief that these writers were lacking in "taste" and in a sense of morality. The novel, as a literary genre, is attacked because it describes passions in themselves, and does not present a moral conclusion. Corneille is approved of in his depiction of passions that are always submissive to a noble morality.

Lautréamont is calling for a repudiation of the hideous part of Romanticism, of the swamplike poetry *(poésie marécageuse)* he feels has undermined the moral fiber of humanity. He uses the harmful effect of absinth, both in a literal sense when speaking of Musset, and in a symbolic sense when speaking of literary works such as Musset wrote. Young pupils in the *lycées* of France are wiser than their teachers when they attack the novels of Balzac and Dumas and Hugo.

School graduation speeches *(discours de distribution pour les lycées)* are the masterpieces of the French language, and a critical appreciation of the works of Voltaire is preferable to the works themselves. Such statements as these are repudiations of all literature in the name of morality. They are expressions of belief that would seem to be impossible to harmonize with *Les Chants de Maldoror.*

Lautréamont singles out Lord Byron, who died at the age of thirty-six at Missolonghi, Greece, as a leading example of a genius who did not use his genius as he should have. In a circuitous meandering passage on Byron, Lautréamont cannot help praising him as one of the four or five "beacons" *(phares)* of humanity, and at the same time he deplores the deliberately cultivated satanism of his work.

Almost as if this contradiction in Byron infuriated him, Lautréamont evokes with the name of Byron, several major "criminals" whom he castigates. At the head of the list is Troppmann, executed in Paris in 1870 for having assassinated a widow and her six children. This crime was one of the most discussed of its day, alluded to by Tourgeniev and Rimbaud. Papavoine, another murderer, killed two children in the Bois de Vincennes. He used a knife and performed the deed in front of their mother. These two historical cases would have been typical of Maldoror, but Lautréamont has now a new set of values. To these two real murderers, Lautréamont has now a new set of values. To these two real murderers, Lautréamont adds several literary heroes: Manfred of Byron, Rodin of Eugène Sue and Sade, Iago of Shakespeare, Colomba of Mérimée. These are grouped with medieval sorcerers, with Prometheus and the Titans of Greek mythology. For Lautréamont they all represent manifestations of evil. He writes here as a Manichean who sees the power of evil predominant in the world.

History is made up of battles and bloodbaths. The fiercest of these were carried out by bulldogs, sharks, and sperm whales *(macrocéphales-cachalots),* all familiar to readers of *Maldoror.* Here Lautréamont interprets his apocalyptic monsters as designating the passions of men, their irreconcilable ambitions, their pride. Is he speaking of himself or is his mind still haunted by the animal symbols of his obsessions? In the midst of the passage he uses such a medical term as "pathological case" *(cas pathologique).* Whether it be a painful or an indulgent reminiscence, his style is once again that of *Les Chants* in its stridency and verboseness.

And yet Lautréamont claims he has expelled from his mind such images and passions, and with them have disappeared all reminiscences of Rousseau and Chateaubriand, of Poe's *Raven,* of Baudelaire's *Une Charogne* and of Jeanne Duval (incorrectly called *la Vénus hottentote* (she was in reality called *la Vénus noire*). By comparison with such "decadent" literature, Lautréamont would write poetry that might be read by a fourteen-year-old girl.

The theme of pain is incompatible with hope. Such seekers after pain as Camoens and Lamartine are childish. Poets of the future must behave otherwise. The inclination to write of sadness leads to despair (as it did in *Confession d'un enfant du siècle* of Musset). This must be avoided because it ends in evil. Musset has, for Lautréamont, a second-rate mind in comparison with the first-rate minds of Lamartine and Hugo. A similar professor-like attributing of grades was being done by Arthur Rimbaud in his *Lettre du voyant* at approximately the same time as Ducasse was writing *Poésies.*

As an extreme case of literature that is opposed to all hope, Lautréamont underscores *Paul et Virginie,* although he does say that if the book by Bernardin de Saint-Pierre were a biography, he would not attack it because then it would represent the will of God. He opposes the creation of disaster in a literary work, as he opposes the treatment of unhappiness as a literary theme. Personal poetry belongs to the past.

Since Racine, poetry has made no progress. It has been travestied by those Lautréamont calls by the curious name *les Grandes-Têtes-Molles de notre époque.* The leading writers are mocked by names such as pupils give to their teachers, in a list that is long and humorous and somewhat reminiscent of Rabelais. George Sand, for example, is called the circumcised hermaphrodite, Théophile Gautier the incomparable grocer, Sénancour the man in feminine attire, Byron the hippopotamus of the infernal jungles.

The Paris Surrealists in the early 1920's enjoyed these vigorous denunciations, although they must have been somewhat puzzled by the inclusion in the list of two writers of Gothic tales whom they looked upon as authentic ancestors of Surrealism: Anne Radcliffe and Maturin.

The final page of *Poésies I* is a specific example drawn from *lycée* classes in which Lautréamont tries to depict the harmful effect on a young mind of Romantic literature of despair. Alfred de Musset again is the object of his wrath. The class *(la troisième)* was given as a subject for a composition a comparison between the pelican episode in *Nuit de mai* and Musset's imitation of himself in his *Lettre à Lamartine* where he uses a farmer *(laboureur)* rather than a pelican, and where death and bloodshed are prevalent. In another class *(la seconde)*, a pupil was asked to translate passages of Pascal and Byron into Hebrew verse. The boy was ill for a month as a result of this labor, and tormented by dreams of horror involving a pelican and a farmer. The cure was in the boy's return to his mother, after days and nights spent in the school's infirmary.

Three brief maxims conclude *Poésies I*. In the first, Lautréamont urges that criticism deal with form rather than content. Pascal is indirectly attacked in the second maxim when Lautréamont says that sentiments are an incomplete form of reasoning (cf. Pascal's *pensée: Tout notre raisonnement se réduit à céder au sentiment*). The third is a paraphrase of Lady Macbeth's famous cry: *Out, out, damned spot. All the perfumes of Arabia*, etc. (V, 1). Romantic sentiment has been altered by an intellectual spot of blood, and all the waters of the sea will not suffice to wash it.

II   Poésies II

Ten brief piercing maxims form the introduction to the second part of *Poésies* and stress the sovereign power of man's reason. Successive editors of the *Poésies* in recent years (Goldfayn and Legrand, Walzer, Marcel Jean) have traced the origin of two of these maxims to Vauvenargues. Two others obviously come from Dante and Shakespeare. In each of these four examples, Lautréamont has changed a word or two in order to recast the maxim in accordance with his desire to praise reason as the protector of sentiments.

The third maxim, for example, "Great thoughts come from man's reason" *(Les grandes pensées viennent de la raison)*, is in opposition to Vauvenargues: *Les grandes pensées viennent du coeur*. In the sixth maxim, "In misfortune, friends grow in number" *(Dans le malheur, les amis augmentent)*, Vauvenargues is again reconstructed: *La prospérité fait peu d'amis*. Here the thought is the same, but the form is made affirmative. Number seven, "You who enter, abandon despair" *(Vous qui entrez, laissez tout désespoir)*, changes Dante's word *speranza* *(Lasciate ogni speranza, voi ch'entrate, Inferno*, Canto III, v. 9). And in maxim eight, "Kindness, your name is man" *(Bonté, ton nom est homme),* Lautréamont alters Hamlet's cry to Ophelia, *"Frailty, thy name is woman"* (I, 2).

Of the ten initial maxims (one constantly thinks in reading this work that the title *Poésies I, II* should be *Pensées* or *Maximes*), the most striking is the second: "Man is not less immortal than the soul" *(L'homme n'est pas moins immortel que l'âme).* Marcel Jean in his edition of Lautréamont, reminds us that André Breton, in commenting on this particular maxim, used a sentence that was written on walls in the Latin Quarter in May, 1968, and which, briefly put, states that man is able to accomplish acts that seem to go beyond his power.

Innumerable passages in *Les Chants* would contradict the fourth maxim: *La fraternité n'est pas un mythe.* The fifth also is in contradiction to Maldoror: "Moral greatness is not innate; it is an acquired virtue. At birth children know nothing about greatness. *Les enfants qui naissent ne connaissent rien de la vie, pas même la grandeur.*

Beginning with the eleventh maxim, the thought is more fully developed, and here Pascal is uppermost in the mind of Lautréamont. The very subject matter of *Les Pensées* is so profound that Pascal was unable to write about it in any sense of order: *J'écrirai ici mes pensées sans ordre. . .* But Lautréamont announces that he will write, with a sense of order, thoughts following one another in logical sequence: *J'écrirai mes pensées avec ordre. . .*

Man is perfect, says Lautréamont. He is not the product of doubt that religions have made him into. Dante and Milton are "hyenas" who have contraverted the truth in their writing. (Rimbaud calls himself *une hyène* in the prefatory page of *Une Saison en enfer.*) Man is an oak tree *(l'homme est un chêne).* With this sentence Lautréamont begins a new version of Pascal's *l'homme est un roseau pensant,* and ends by calling the universe a "thinking reed." In a plethora of literary allusions, Lautréamont strives to prove that romantic and quasi-religious poses demean the dignity of man: Lamartine as lover of Graziella, Musset as lover of George Sand, Chateaubriand's rock tomb in the sea at Saint-Malo, Poe's study where the raven appeared nightly.

In his contradistinctions to the past, both immediate and distant, Lautréamont invokes Pascal more frequently than other writers. Man's greatness, he says, comes from his recognition of being great and not in being miserable, as Pascal would claim. By writing out his thoughts, Lautréamont prevents them from disappearing. Man's heart is a book he has learned to esteem. But man is not mysterious, he is not fallen, he is not imperfect. The monstrousness of man that Pascal had described, *Quelle chimère est-ce donc que l'homme?* is contradicted by Lautréamont in minute detail. Whereas Pascal calls man *un monstre incompréhensible,* Lautréamont insists there is nothing incomprehensible in the world. *Il n'y a rien d'incompréhensible.* It is a maxim extensively applauded and used by the Surrealists.

When Lautréamont defines poetry as the revelation of truth, which will have a practical purpose in the conduct of human affairs, we can see reasons for calling these moralistic maxims *Poésies.* He envisages the poet as the most practical member of the tribe. However, the real poets of civilization were not Homer or Vergil, but rather Socrates and Christ.

In the French classical age, poets and philosophers were in accord with one another: Racine and Descartes, for example. But in the nineteenth century, a dichotomy exists between the poets, between Hugo, for example, and such a philosopher as Hippolyte Taine, whose *Traité de l'Intelligence* had just appeared in 1870, and which is named by Lautréamont. He calls Hugo's plays *vaudevilles barbares* and praises the plays of Racine and Corneille as proclaiming man's duty to the world and to himself.

Literary problems hold Lautréamont only as long as he discusses them in terms of morality. He easily moves to abstract thoughts on morality, as when he simplifies the dogma of grace by saying that the only grace there is is that of being born. After passages closely related to Pascal, Lautréamont returns to pure moralists: La Rochefoucauld, La Bruyère and Vauvenargues, whose name appears several times.

The two critics Marcel Jean and Arpad Mezei believe that the socio-philosophical arguments of Proudhon were widely used by Lautréamont. The thought of Proudhon who was anti-religious, anti-theistic, anti-Romantic, does coincide at several points with Lautréamont. At the time of Lautréamont it is quite true that the system of Proudhon was more studied in France than the system of Karl Marx (of which there is no trace in Lautréamont.)

Lautréamont refuses to separate the study of abstract sciences from the study of man. He found more companions engaged in the study of man than in the study of geometry. This passage, beginning *J'avais passé beaucoup de temps dans l'étude des sciences abstraites,* is diametrically opposed to Pascal's *pensée* beginning with identical words. In a maxim on justice, by changing two words in a maxim of La Rochefoucauld, Lautréamont declares that the law of justice is the courage to bear injustice.

In increasingly strong terms. and by a rewriting of famous passages in French literature, Lautréamont repudiates *Les Chants de Maldoror.* He scorns both Romantic poets and Romantic heroes, and raises the critic, the appreciative moralist, above the poet. The analysis of sentiment which Lautréamont calls the function of the critic, prevents any overt expression of sentimentalizing, although it possesses a latent sensibility. Throughout these passages, Lautréamont is constantly opposing youth to maturity, which equates the opposition of sentimentality to the power of reasoning. When this is cast in terms of literary genres, it implies the shift from tragedies, poems, elegies, to the calculated coldness of maxims. *Primera la froideur de la maxime.* Lautréamont finds that he cannot name a moralist who is a first-rate poet.

It is at this point in his disquisition that Lautréamont writes the maxim which, thanks to the Surrealists, has become his best-known sentence: "Poetry must be made by everyone. Not by one man." *(La poésie doit être faite par tous. Non par un.)* He lists the names of six poets, all preceded by the adjective "poor": *Pauvre Hugo! Pauvre Racine!* etc., and ends the sentence with the word *tics,* repeated three times. *Tic,* referring to a facial twinge or characteristic mania, helps to explain the opening remark.

The Romantic wanted to be individualistic, each characterized by themes or obsessions, by traits that would identify them. Such deliberate identifications should give way to instinctive expressions characteristic of all men, expressions that all men could utter and in which they would recognize themselves. The great revelations of men rise up from their subconscious. The subconscious would therefore be a leveling, egalitarian process. Like Rimbaud, Lautréamont believed that the writer, the real creator, has not yet come into the world. Each of these youthful writers, in his own way, in his own solitude, was the voice in the wilderness announcing the spirit to come who will liberate mankind from conventions and prejudices and literary genres.

Prayer to the Almighty is useless, says Lautréamont. He is fully aware of his own greatness. The best way to show gratitude to God is to love humanity, to treat other men as one's brothers. There is no need to study evil in order to bring out or emphasize the good. As his arguments continue, Lautréamont elevates the poet above other writers, but that is because the poet is in the moralist and the philosopher. Struggling against evil is honoring it too much.

At this point, which is close to the end of *Poésies II,* Lautréamont, in a strict sequence, rewrites seventeen *pensées* of Pascal, thirty *maximes* of Vauvenargues and one *maxime* of La Bruyère. These passages, so transcribed and altered that they are made to testify to an optimistic attitude toward man's nature and motivations, form the conclusion of Lautréamont's work. Very few words are changed in each passage, but they are the key words giving to the *pensée* or *maxime* a new meaning that is steadfastly affirmative. If Pascal says, "it would be good if the laws were obeyed," Lautréamont says, "it is good the laws are obeyed." If Vauvenargues says, "despair is our greatest error," Lautréamont says, "despair is our smallest error."

Poésies is a curious work and doubtless would have been transitional if Lautréamont had lived. It corresponds to the attitude of the young writer who, unappreciated, turns against literature and denounces his forerunners. Rimbaud was writing his first poems when Lautréamont was writing *Poésies,* and Rimbaud, too, was to attack literature in the same way, denounce some of the same authors, and finally abandon the career of writer. If Ducasse had not died, he might well have entered upon the same silence that characterized the last years of Rimbaud. They both revealed a typical youthful temperament of spitefulness and bitter disappointment, and even anger. Both had yearned for recognition and literary fame. Both had striven to startle and impress the established literary figures of the day. Both were ignored, and both gave up an avant-garde position. Lautréamont, in *Poésies* returned to a moralistic view of literature as being a means to reach the good life. Rimbaud, in his voyage to Africa, entered upon a practical life of commerce and trade.

CHAPTER 5

Lautréamont and His Critics

F ROM the beginning, critics were unwilling to grant full literary rights to Lautréamont. Had he not been insane, or at least partially insane? He dealt with forms of eroticism and perversion associated with Sade. And then there was no available biography upon which to base and explain the moral, social, and philosophical development of the writer. Genonceaux, in his edition of 1890, gathered the first bits biographical information, but they were exterior facts and not at all dependable. In 1970, François Caradec published his biography of Lautréamont. He had carefully investigated all that could be investigated, and provided information concerning the voyages possible and real of Isidore Ducasse between South America and Europe, and information on the various hotels in which he lived in Paris. In a word, almost nothing that would help a critic in his analysis of the work itself.

In addition to all that, the work is difficult to break down into themes. There are almost no characters and no characterizations. There is no recognizable structure or plot. The elements of plot, structure, and characters are there but appear in so confused a state that, again, the work fits no obvious category.

Such a book as Lautréamont's has gained little from traditional criticism, but is now entering upon a new era with the advent of newer forms of criticism and new movements in art and literature. Psychoanalysis and Surrealism and the newest approaches of structuralist criticism have opened up the way to a fresh understanding. Until recently *Les Chants de Maldoror* had usually been interpreted in its analogies with the Gothic tale *(le roman noir),* with the popular horror novel, and with the more strident rhetoric of Romanticism. Today the work does not appear easier to read. There are still many mysteries in it, but a few of the new critics who have paid very careful attention to it have provided clues that will help in future criticism: Bachelard, Blanchot, Jean-Pierre Weber, and Philippe Sollers.

There are certain constant traits throughout the writings of

Lautréamont that make it possible to speak of his "world," as recognizable as that of Mallarmé or of Saint-John Perse. But other traits appear inconsistent or paradoxical. At times, for example, his fictional narrative seems grimly serious, but then he intervenes in his story in order to deride his fiction and to deride all fiction, for that matter. Whatever Lautréamont takes seriously, he makes fun of. Perhaps that trait in itself is a constant.

The work holds up today largely because of the emotion it creates in some readers (although that emotion is not as intense as it was for early Surrealists), and for the fascination it exercises over such writers as Henri Michaux and Jean-Marie Le Clézio. The newest criticism has been a psychoanalysis of Lautréamont based upon his writings and not upon his life. It is therefore largely a consideration of Lautréamont in his relationship with language. Why did he write? Why did he write as he did?

All criticism, both traditional and new, is an effort to make clear or explicit what is unclear or implicit in a work. A history of the critical studies on Lautréamont would also be a history of French criticism between 1890 and 1973. What follows a literary work in history as well as in literary history changes the meaning of the work.

I *Earliest Critics: 1868–1885*

Between 1868 (publication date of the first canto) and 1885, only one critical article appeared, in a little magazine, *La Jeunesse.* The article was signed by Epistémon who may have been the editor of the magazine, Alfred Sircos. To describe the effect of the reading on him, Epistémon used the word *étonnement* (surprise). And then he analyzed *étonnement* by such terms as "bombast," "hyperbole," "wild strangeness," and commended such traits as being a welcome change from the pallid dull publications of the day. The sickness of Maldoror he related to *le mal du siècle,* as spoken of by Alfred de Musset. Maldoror is thus related to Byron's Childe Harold and Goethe's Faust with the themes of uncertainty over the future, despair, scorn for the past, incredulity.

These first points, made by Epistémon, were all cogent and were utilized by critics coming after him. A brief note appearing in *La Jeune Belgique,* in 1885, called attention to the fact that there were still readers of *Les Chants de Maldoror.* Two articles by Gérard

Bauër and Maurice Saillet, in 1954, established evidence that it was Max Waller, founder of *La Jeune Belgique* who, in 1885, bought the copies of the edition of 1869 that had never been put on sale, and sent out personal copies to Léon Bloy, Huysmans and others, in order to call attention to Lautréamont.

II *1887–1919: Bloy, Gourmont, Larbaud, Breton*

Bauër reported in his article (*Le Figaro Littéraire*, 27 Feb. 1954) that it was Waller who initiated the legend of Lautréamont's madness. In his novel of 1887, *Le Désespéré*, Léon Bloy spoke briefly of Lautréamont. His long article, the first extensive writing on Lautréamont, was published in *La Plume*, September, 1890, and entitled, *Le Cabanon de Prométhée*.

Today the style of Léon Bloy's writing seems more bombastic, more inflated than that of Lautréamont. He described first the appeal of ruins, the association with the past and with death that the contemplation of ruins calls up. Then he referred to another kind of ruin, that of a human life, the ruin of a man of genius. This was Lautréamont whose *Chants de Maldoror* appeared to Bloy as a monstrous production. "The author of this book died in a hovel *(cabanon)* and that is all we know about him."

He announces that the satanism of *Les Fleurs du Mal* seems mild by comparison. But despite the absence of literary form—the text is a "liquid lava"—the work will appeal and sell widely, he predicts. Bloy refers to the blasphemies he finds in *Les Chants* in order to speak of the blasphemous age in which he is living. Every point he makes is to underscore the abnormality and insanity of Lautréamont, and hence the incoherence of his writing.

Rémy de Gourmont also referred to the madness of Lautréamont in an article of 1891, reprinted in *Le Livre des masques,* and in 1920 in an introduction to a new edition of *Les Chants*. He drew his conclusions from the text rather than from inaccurate biographical information. He analyzed the suffering of Lautréamont as *la folie de la persécution.* Gourmont unquestionably admired the work. It was he who discovered the existence of the *Poésies* of Isidore Ducasse in the Bibliothèque Nationale.

There were very few other references to Lautréamont before 1920: a few remarks by Huysmans and Gustave Kahn, and a short study by a Nicaraguan poet Rubén Darío, in his book *Los raros,* published in Barcelona in 1908. During the years between his death and 1920, Lautréamont was read mainly by writers. This had been true also of Sade throughout the nineteenth century.

An article of Valery Larbaud in *La Phalange,* of Feb. 20, 1914, reminded his readers of the existence of the two small pamphlets of *Poésies* in the Bibliothèque Nationale. The work was finally published by André Breton in the second and third issues of his magazine *Littérature: Poésies I* in April, 1919, and *Poésies II* in May, 1919.

III *1920–1929: Malraux, Gide, Breton, Pierre-Quint*

The year 1920 was the turning point in the fortunes of Lautréamont. *Poésies* appeared in book form with a preface by Philippe Soupalt. A new edition of *Les Chants* was brought out in Paris by Les éditions La Sirène, and André Malraux published in *Action* the *variantes* of the first canto: *La genèse des Chants de Maldoror* (April, 1920). Then began the period of increasing admiration for Lautréamont felt by Gide, for example, and by all of the young Surrealists.

Malraux's article is curious in the sense that the critic is struck by the originality of Lautréamont, by the English sources of the work, and by the poet's habit of transposing abstractions into names of objects or animals; and yet he seems irritated by his own interest in the work. He concludes, somewhat feebly, that Lautréamont was too young to have written an important work, that a major writer expresses the experiences of a lifetime!

The three young Surrealists who directed *Littérature,* André Breton, Louis Aragon and Philippe Soupault, were the first critics responsible for calling attention to Lautréamont and for insisting upon the importance of his work. And André Gide, in his turn, was the first to praise the Surrealists for having recognized the literary and extraliterary significance of Lautréamont. His article was published in a special edition of *Le Disque Vert,* in 1925. Gide spoke of the strange power in Lautréamont which he found to be without precedent in French literature. And in prophetic vein, he announced that Lautréamont with Rimbaud, and perhaps more than Rimbaud, will be the master of the sluices *(écluses)* for the new literature to come.

Gide had declined an invitation to write the preface for an edition of Lautréamont, and justified himself by implying that *Les Chants* is a book for initiates and needs no preface. He had already associated Lautréamont with Rimbaud in two entries of his *Journal* of November, 1905. At that time he had felt shame for the excessive literariness of his own writing, by comparison with the vigor and boldness of Rimbaud and Lautréamont, which he believed to be due to their less extensive literary culture.

In his final sentence of the brief text of 1925, Gide was an accurate prophet: *il est le maître des écluses pour la littérature de demain.* In Soupault's preface to the 1920 edition of *Les chants de Maldoror,* the Surrealist veneration began to be expressed. The entire issue of the Franco-Belgian publication, *Le Disque Vert,* in which Gide's article appeared, was devoted to Lautréamont. In this general homage—the issue was called *Le cas Lautréamont*—young Surrealists (Soupault and René Crevel) appeared with more established writers: Jules Supervielle, Ungaretti, Maeterlinck, Cocteau, Jean Paulhan.

Such was the veneration of the Surrealists that they were indignant with themselves for giving Lautréamont over to the annals of literature, for revealing his work to readers unworthy of him. His was a sacred text that should be kept for the "happy few." The Surrealists continued to feel this way and opposed every effort to allocate Lautréamont to a given category in literary history. In his negation of all sociableness, of all human constraints, Lautréamont went far beyond literature, according to the Surrealists. Breton, who easily castigated those he had once approved, never flinched in his admiration for Lautréamont, who remained the sacred prophet for the new world the Surrealists believed would come. In his preface to the *Oeuvres complètes* of 1938, Breton calls *Les Chants de Maldoror* the definitive apocalypse.

However, despite the desire of Breton and the other Surrealists to keep Lautréamont as a sacred text for themselves, the first important critical study appeared in 1929, *Le comte de Lautréamont et Dieu* by Léon Pierre-Quint. This book initiated what is now a long series of critical studies, each one of which emphasizes a theory concerning Lautréamont or an approach to his writings. Pierre-Quint analyzes in particular Maldoror's revolt against God. Lautréamont's hero, intoxicated with his love for evil, finds his greatest satisfaction in sadistic acts. Whenever Maldoror feels and expresses tenderness and compassion, such sentiments seem directed toward adolescents. And yet, he is able, through some deep-seated exasperation, to turn his violence on them too. Léon Pierre-Quint asks the leading question: What is the meaning of this revolt? He calls it the intellectual revolt *(révolte de l'esprit)* that follows the absolutistic revolt of adolescence *(révolte absolue)*.

In his analysis of Lautréamont's humor, Léon Pierre-Quint makes him into a forerunner of our contemporary form of humor, as seen especially in the theater of the absurd. The effects of parody and humor are attempts, on the part of Lautréamont, to belittle man, to reveal the ridiculousness of his pretensions and his conventions. Lautréamont's antiliterature attitude is the announcement of Dada. His humor is therefore a part of his revolt against the human spirit and art. At the end of his study, Léon Pierre-Quint expresses the conviction that Lautréamont had reached a belief that could be called total nihilism. With such a philosophy, his mysterious disappearance from the earth at the age of twenty-four would make good sense. After more than forty years, this early book of Pierre-Quint remains one of the most serious and illuminating studies on Lautréamont.

IV 1939–1963: Bachelard, Jean and Mezei, Weber, Blanchot

Ten years later, in 1939, Gaston Bachelard published his short study of Lautréamont, revised and enlarged in an edition of 1963. This book served many years as the standard psychoanalytical treatment of Lautréamont. Bachelard calls *Les Chants de Maldoror* a phenomenology of aggression, and studies in particular what he calls the "complex of animal life" in the work. By using the entire animal world, he is able to present evil as something total. He studies the bestiary of Lautréamont and describes the various animal organs that serve the impulse of aggression. The claw *(la griffe)* he finds to be the symbol of pure will. Those animals that suck blood, *la ventouse*, such as the spider, bloodsucker, tarantula, vampire, octopus, represent the other major type of attack. By use of the animal kingdom, Lautréamont has been able to make the vices of man concrete. Although there are many forms of revolt in *Les Chants*, Bachelard finds that the most violent of them all, the most intransigent, is the adolescent revolt against the world.

Bachelard was the first critic to express strong opposition to the theory, advanced by Léon Bloy and Rémy de Gourmont, that Lautréamont was insane. The power of his verbal expression and the coherence of the work contradicted such a theory. Bachelard proposed the opposite theory: Lautréamont had been able to dominate and sublimate whatever fantasies beset him.

In 1947, the book of Marcel Jean and Arpad Mezei, *Les Chants de Maldoror, essai sur Lautréamont,* provided not only a further psychoanalytical approach to Lautréamont, but also a commentary on the occult in his work. These young critics placed emphasis on the dream sequences in the *chants* that are interpreted as those of a child brutally separated from his family. To support a secondary thesis, they found traces of a friendship, possibly a love-friendship that had been betrayed and that had helped sharpen the bitterness and violence of Lautréamont's revolt. Because of Maldoror's multiple metamorphoses and his ability to move so swiftly from place to place, his ubiquity, his elusiveness, Jean and Mezei identified him with Satan.

Like Bachelard, these younger critics find coherence in Lautréamont, and moreover, a definite form and progression in the narrative. They interpret the first canto as representing the prenatal life; Cantos II and III as the revolt of the world against the father; Cantos IV and V as the development of the self with emphasis on the genital life. Canto VI is the most purely narrative, the story canto which concludes with the death of Mervyn. The work thus depicts the entire human experience, beginning with prenatal life and continuing until death. Marcel Jean and Arpad Mezei have presented the most original and speculative theories concerning the names of Maldoror and Lautréamont. *Mald* (from *maudit*) and *oror* (from *aurore*), or "accursed light" would refer to Lucifer (or "light-bearer"). In "Lautréamont," the critics see *l'autre Amon,* or Amon Râ, the Egyptian sun god or the sun of hermeticism. The six cantos would be the six operations of the philosophical stone.

In an article more purely psychiatric than the writings of Marcel Jean and Arpad Mezei, Yvonne Rispal considers *Les Chants* as the epic story of the couple, of the schizophrenic struggle between the man Isidore Ducasse and the poet comte de Lautréamont. This analysis, appearing in the October, 1962, issue of *Cahiers du Groupe Françoise Minkowska,* describes the cohabitation of the imaginative power of Ducasse and the shrewd intelligence of Lautréamont.

But a divorce took place, and at the end of the narrative, the weaker of the two (Ducasse) left the stronger, who then settled into an ultimate form of solitude.

Jean-Paul Weber devotes a chapter in his book *Domaines thématiques* (1963) to *Les Chants de Maldoror,* in which he studies what he considers the basic theme of the work, namely masturbation. The name *mal d'aurore* would designate the act of masturbation at the beginning of the day, provoked by the sexual fantasies of the adolescent. The many references to blood, saliva, and droolings come from a fundamental obsession which makes the work resemble a flow and liquid propulsion. Weber feels the passages on aggressiveness, resentment, remorse relate to the images of masturbation. The violence against God, against man and woman, the heroes and villains, the instruments of torture—all these bear relationship with a child's world of revolt and the release found in masturbation.

Dr. Jean-Pierre Soulier's book, *Lautréamont génie ou maladie mentale* (1964), is a psychiatrist's attempt to interpret *Les Chants* as a work coming from an extreme form of schizophrenia, and even more precisely than that, from a paranoid form of schizophrenia. This critic finds that the scenes of cruel atrocities are narrated in a tone of such cool detachment that there is an evident split between the horror of the story and the serene attitude of the storyteller. Soulier calls particular attention to the use of the mirror in the work, and the habit of the schizophrenic to remain immobilized in front of a mirror and watch the reflected image which he does not associate with himself.

Soulier opposes the theory that his psychopathological interpretation of *Les Chants* would relegate the work to an inferior category of artistic achievement. He points out, as in the cases of Dostoevski, Van Gogh, Antonin Artaud, that we do not expect from the artist anything that resembles a normally lived life. Everything that Lautréamont wrote was deliberately created and carefully organized. This is typical behavior in the schizophrene and the paranoid.

Because the many violent and varied images in *Les Chants* always reveal Lautréamont himself in the center of the action and the imagery, Paul Zweig, in his study, *Lautréamont ou les violences du Narcisse* (1967), sees Lautréamont as a new type of Narcissus, not the languorous adolescent of the myth, but the defiant revolutionary of modern times, the immediate precursor of the "angry young men" and the "freaks." The scenes of violence are intended to break down the boundaries and release the perpetrator of violence to a life of greater freedom. And yet such scenes, according to Zweig, take place in a closed-in area.

By multiplying his metamorphoses, Maldoror-Lautréamont is teaching his reader, treating him both as a pupil and a victim. His ever-increasing violence is the underscoring of the teacher's role. His language becomes *crétinisation,* as Lautréamont says, an effort to dull and stupefy the mind of the reader. This is also the will to self-destruction. The episodes are attempts on the part of Lautréamont to defeat himself. The bombastic revolt ends by being a humiliating failure.

As Narcissus sought to see himself, so Maldoror seeks to find his identity. The copulation with the female shark is a clue to this search for Zweig. Whereas Narcissus tried to see himself on the surface of the water, Maldoror plunges below the surface into the depths of the water and accomplishes there a scene of incest, since the sea is the mother-image.

Zweig lists four major enemies whom Maldoror must overcome in order to see himself and find himself: nature, men, the Creator, and himself. In his struggle against God (and here Zweig's thesis resembles that of Léon Pierre-Quint), Maldoror appears as the son in his attempt to defeat the father. It is the masculine counterpart of the incest drama in the shark episode. Violent passions are endlessly aroused in Maldoror's search for identity, in the narcissistic hope of discovering a resemblance with himself. But in seeing himself as the wayward son, he becomes the father, or at least he resembles the father by appropriating all the paternal prestige. In struggling with the Almighty, Maldoror rises to the divine eminence.

Three writers, usually grouped with the "new" French critics, in keeping with the precepts of the new criticism, avoid any historical approach to Lautréamont, and any emphasis on literary sources and biography. Each of these critics has his own method, but all three look upon the text of Lautréamont as autonomous, as a literary expression that can be studied in terms of its formal aspects.

Maurice Blanchot's study of *Lautréamont et Sade,* 1949, still appears today as one of the truly significant critical appraisals.

Lautréamont serves Blanchot as a means for discussing the tentative provisional characteristics of all criticism, and the need in literary criticism to separate a given work from all other works of its age, and see it solely in itself. He points out that if Lautréamont was indeed well read (*son imagination est entourée de livres*), he was not a "bookish" writer, and that a mere study of the literary sources of *Maldoror* would not explain the power of the work. The critic found so much ambivalence in the themes of *Les Chants* that he gave up the possibility of applying thematic criticism to Lautréamont.

In describing his method of approach, Blanchot described what today is looked upon as structuralist criticism. Rather than studying what is expressed directly, he wanted to study what is behind the text. He studied not the images themselves in the finished work, but possible reasons for Lautréamont's choice of the images. How is it possible to explain Lautréamont's preference for certain kinds of images? The constant attack on God, for example, is not as important, according to Blanchot, as the fantasy animal images which these attacks inevitably call forth.

Blanchot believes that the act of writing a work changed Lautréamont. As the work was being devised and written, its own logic was imposed on the writer, and he grew into a changed human being. In Canto I, the passage on the ocean, its violence and tensions are such that Lautréamont himself must have needed time and perspective to understand its significance. If such a passage appears powerful in its form, the sentiments that lie behind its form are even more powerful. What is, for example, the hypnotic power of the simple word *le mal,* used in Canto I? What was the truth of such a word for Lautréamont? It must have had a deeply personal meaning, concealed or half-concealed in the past of Isidore Ducasse.

As stanza succeeded stanza, problems, experiences, and obsessions rose up from the past of the writer's experience, were recorded in terms of an image or a fantasy narrative, and then sank back again into the past. This would account for the seeming discontinuity of the composition. In a few episodes (I:11; II:16; and especially V:7) Blanchot believes this lucidity concerning the past became so strong that Lautréamont was paralyzed by it and had to refuse to write out a complete transcription. In the second canto in particular, where the theme of childhood is recurrent, Lautréamont dilates between aggressiveness and passivity. There he attempts, but futilely, to establish the theme of love for a youth. He is thwarted every time the theme forces itself upon his imagination and his memory. The defiance addressed to God comes in part from the belief that God does not want Maldoror to break through the limits of his consciousness and thereby reach a fuller lucidity concerning the dramas of his life.

Blanchot emphasizes the beginning of Canto IV where he sees a change in language coming from a greater violence of disorder in thinking and striving to think. Maldoror is walled in by his intelligence (*l'homme et moi, claquemurés dans les limites de notre intelligence*). It is the passage where Maldoror says he continues to exist like basalt. His permanence seems indestructible, his existence petrified. It is the obsession of disintegration and enslavement. Maldoror has failed in every effort to reach a fraternal union.

In his analysis of the two movements of metamorphosis, extreme violence on the one hand, and extreme passivity on the other, Blanchot finds them equally powerful, equally important in Maldoror's search for self-knowledge. The freedom Maldoror is seeking is the freedom from his memories and especially from the nostalgia for his childhood he continues to feel. Much of the work is a long night, an intolerable nightmare culminating in what Blanchot calls a *dénouement* at the end of Canto V. But there the coming of daylight is ironic. What has been won is paltry. The freedom reached in the *dénouement* is a form of abdication. The morning of the new day is a twilight, and the feelings of Maldoror are apathy and fatigue.

Blanchot's thesis centers on the omnipotence of evil in Lautréamont. The only force that was not evil in Lautréamont was his consciousness of it. Even the act of writing was inevitably the writer's act of taking sides with evil.

Blanchot's study is more complete than that of Marcelin Pleynet or of Philippe Sollers, both of whom have applied structuralist methods to their critical writings on Lautréamont.

V *1967–1968: Pleynet, Sollers*

In his book *Lautréamont par lui-même* (1967), Marcelin Pleynet reviews not so much the content of the Gothic novels, as the form they suggested to Lautréamont in the dualism they announced of good and evil. The antagonism between passions and morals is expressed metaphorically by Lautréamont is his use of the "forest," for example, which contains the debate or struggle between banditry and innocence. The same kind of counterpoint is visible in the "ocean" where the struggle lies between a storm and man's courage. In the metaphor of the "sky," one can read the opposition between storm and peace. The subject of this contrapuntal repetition is Lautréamont himself. He is the permanent site of the activities and the debates over good and evil. There is no need, for this structuralist critic, to study the biographical evidence and the literary sources in *Les Chants de Maldoror*. The book does not say more than what it says.

Basing his argument on the opening line of *Les Chants (Plût au ciel que le lecteur, enhardi et. . .)*, Pleynet develops the thesis that an extraordinary relationship exists between the writer and the reader. As the narration continues, the critic finds that one becomes identified with the other. The relationship between reader and writer is a form of incest, and here again Pleynet calls upon the opening lines of the work where Lautréamont speaks of the danger of his work and the need for the timid reader to turn away from contemplation (and desire) of his mother.

Philippe Sollers, in his article *La science de Lautréamont*, published in *Critique* (October, 1965), and reprinted in *Logiques* (1968), considers *Les Chants de Maldoror* a "psychography" because, in addition to the continuing narrative line of the work, many other matters are being studied simultaneously. Sollers, one of the most difficult of the new critics in France, sees in the "ocean" passage a study of the human heart that is more profound than the customary ideological writing about the heart. He sees *Les Chants* as a text that reveals an important interpretation of homosexuality. Rather than being a transgression against the law, he finds it to be the realization of the law, in its obsession with the phallus, not only in the erotic sense, but as the clue to civilization: knowledge, truth, man, father, Creator.

VI *Homage Issues*

The critics today have in nowise heeded the early cry of the Surrealists who asked that no critic approach the work of Lautréamont. The text was too sacred to allow incompetent interpretation and unholy maulings. During the past twelve years, since approximately 1960, some of the most subtle critical minds in France have examined closely the texts of Lautréamont in efforts to understand what can be understood about literature. Out of a text so variously interpreted, the new critics have discovered one that seems to them fully self-conscious and fully lucid. It is primarily a seminal book, not one composed in accordance with recognizable rules governing a poem or a narrative. Two magazines recently have devoted entire issues to Lautréamont: *L'Arc* in 1967 and *Entretiens* in 1971.

The director of *Entretiens,* Max Chaleil, in his introduction article finds that in both *Les Chants* and *Poésies,* Lautréamont is proposing a new order of the world. Donato Pelayo's article, *L'homme aux lèvres de soufre,* concludes, as did many of the earlier critics, that evil is the central problem in *Les Chants,* but that evil has been exorcised by the work. The practice of evil is self-destructive and corrosive. The power of Lautréamont's writing is the depiction of man's life in an aggressive nature. A single man's adventure is in reality the collective adventure of the species. The language of Lautréamont was not tempered by all the civilizing forces that control most literary works. His writing is close to the primitive songs of humanity.

The final article in *Entretiens,* by Frans de Haes, is a comparison of the Surrealists' approach to Lautréamont, with the newer approach represented by the critics associated with the magazine *Tel Quel.* Frans de Haes accuses the Surrealists of verbal inflation and vagueness when writing about Lautréamont, and praises the *Tel Quel* critics: Sollers, Derrida, Lacan, among others, for their greater precision and penetration. But in grouping Lautréamont with such writers as the marquis de Sade, Antonin Artaud and Georges Bataille, the *Tel Quel* critics are inflating the importance of these writers and may fall into the same temptations of the Surrealists.

The Corti edition of the *Oeuvres complètes* has published the various prefaces to other editions of Lautréamont. In each case the preface was written by a distinguished critic: Edmond Jaloux, Rémy de Gourmont, André Breton, Roger Caillois, Philippe Soupault, Maurice Blanchot, Julien Gracq. The commentaries, some very brief, of the Surrealists would make a significant study in itself, and testify to an important aspect of critical writing on Lautréamont: Tristan Tzara, Philippe Soupault, René Crevel, Paul Eluard. A close examination of such texts would reveal greater divergence of opinion among the Surrealists than is usually believed to exist.

VII Briefer Studies: Miller, Artaud, Camus, Césaire, Le Clézio

In addition to the serious book-length studies on Lautréamont and the above-mentioned articles, five additional and independent articles appear worthy of study. They were written by men who have been attentive to Lautréamont for different reasons, most of which were personal.

In the fall, 1944, issue of *Accent,* a now defunct literary magazine published in Urbana, Illinois, Henry Miller contributed an article for which he used as a title a phrase from Canto IV, Stanza 7: "Let us be content with three little new-born elephants." The passage leads into the sentence on the two neighboring monarchs, Maldoror and God. Writing in the same style that characterizes his pages on Rimbaud and D. H. Lawrence, Miller adds personal jibes and quips to his principal argument. He states that the Anglo-Saxon temperament with its love for violence and pornography and cruelty, may one day make *Les Chants de Maldoror* a best-seller. The Judge Woolsey decision in favor of Joyce's *Ulysses* against the United States, made 1933 a banner year in the war waged on censorship, and opened up the way to the publication of such works as those of Lautréamont and Sade. Part of the battle against literary hypocrisy was won. Henceforth, simple direct language, including the four-letter words, could be used by writers. The three sinister-looking stars of the nineteenth century, Baudelaire, Rimbaud and Lautréamont, would be sufficient to make it one of the most illustrious literary centuries. There were other major writers, of course: Whitman, Blake, Dostoevski, Kierkegaard and Nietzsche, but the three "bandits," as Miller calls Baudelaire, Rimbaud and Lautréamont, have been sanctified in a very special way. They were angels in disguise.

Henry Miller points out the beginning of Canto IV as being something unique in literature, "A man or a stone or a tree is going to begin this canto" *(C'est un homme ou une pierre ou un arbre qui va commencer le 4e chant).* Such a sentence, although written in French, goes beyond French literature toward something that seems rather to appear Aztec-like, Patagonian-like. Miller refers to the passage on God's hair left in the bordello, and the lovemaking scene between the female shark and Maldoror. The moment in history when Lautréamont lived was so sad that the genius had to rise above it, like a bird in the air, like an albatross. The literary genres, with their precise definitions and forms, have little meaning when applied to Lautréamont. An analysis of the themes and scaffoldings in *Les Chants* will do little good. What counts, says Miller, is the fact that a man is crucifying himself in the work. Tenderness and humility are also there. In speaking directly to his reader, Miller says that if you have never taken a trip to nadir, here is your chance.

The monstrousness of Lautréamont's dream is more real for Miller than the imbecilic acts of man's daily life. The absolute evil sung by Lautréamont and perpetrated by Maldoror is more pure than the devious counterfeit forms of evil that we encounter each day. The reading of Lautréamont is therapeutic for Henry Miller. It provides a clearing of the air, a means by which we may see in perspective the dual role throughout history of the two monarchs, of God and man.

In a more violent language than Henry Miller's, Antonin Artaud, just prior to his death, published in the *Cahiers du Sud* issue on Lautréamont (August, 1946) a short article, *"Lettre sur Lautréamont."* Artaud used the occasion to vituperate against the narrowness of the bourgeois mind, on the necessary mask worn by the young man Isidore Ducasse who became in his writing the "unthinkable" count, *le comte impensable de Lautréamont.* Artaud undoubtedly identified himself with the career and the suffering of Lautréamont as he underscored the abyss that inevitably lies between the genius and the world surrounding him.

The litany of names he recites, Poe, Nerval, Baudelaire, Rimbaud, to whom he added Nietzsche and Van Gogh, are those artists who were not assimilated by the world, who in their vision of artist were alienated. Today we would not hesitate to place Artaud himself in

such a list. Artaud repeats the list at the end of his article and contrasts that type of "irreducible" genius with the other type who
became the spokesman of his age, who was not opposed to his age:
Hugo, Lamartine, Musset, Chateaubriand. Rather than calling him
a visionary, or a man hallucinated, Artaud calls him the genius who
saw clearly and realistically into his life and who stirred up the
fires of his subconscious. For Artaud, Lautréamont died of rage
over wanting to preserve his intrinsic individuality.

In *L'homme révolté* (1951), Albert Camus studied, among other
matters, that kind of metaphysical revolt which is purely negative.
The poetry of revolt that appeared in Europe at the end of the
nineteenth and the early part of the twentieth century, vacillated,
according to Camus, between the irrational and the rational,
between a form of desperate nihilistic dream and determined
action. Those who in their art attacked the order of heaven, were,
in reality, demonstrating a deep-seated longing for order. They
were the immediate heirs of Romanticism and sought to discover
under the hypocrisy and conventions of their day, what they called
"real life," *la vraie vie*. Poetry thus became for them experiment
and action. Camus named Rimbaud and Lautréamont the leading
experimentalists. He emphasized their youthfulness in the portrait
they give of a man's revolt (*la révolte*). The contradictions in Lautréamont are pathetically those of a youth attacking the creation
and attacking himself. As principal contradiction, Camus points
out that on the one hand Lautréamont says he has come to defend
man *(Je me présente pour défendre l'homme)* and on the other
hand, he exclaims: "Show me a man who is good" *(Montre-moi
un homme qui soit bon)*. This alternating positive and negative
attitude represents for Camus the nihilistic type of revolt. The
hero Maldoror, in his conventional black cloak, is the rebel, and
moreover, for Camus, he is the metaphysical dandy who, because
he despairs of divine justice, will go over to the side of evil. His
plan is quite simply to cause suffering in others, and to suffer
himself. With God as his enemy, Maldoror is intoxicated with the
power of master criminals: *moi seul contre l'humanité*.

Camus follows the thought of Maurice Blanchot in separating
Canto I from the others. Published separately, Canto I reproduces
Byronic commonplaces, whereas the other cantos contain the real
drama of Lautréamont and the theme of the monster. If the typical

Romantic emphasized the solitude of the genius and the indifference of God (Vigny, for example), and used as graphic representation of this solitude the isolated castle (Combourg for Chateaubriand) and the pose of the dandy (Musset and Baudelaire), Lautréamont went farther in his revolt by wishing to efface all frontiers between God and man. The supreme revolt would be the blotting out simultaneously of man and the world. Camus argues that the creatures in *Les Chants* are all amphibians because Maldoror refuses the world as it is with its limitations and demarcations. The critic sees the ocean, so richly orchestrated as a theme by Lautréamont, to be symbol of both reconciliation and annihilation. Pascal's admonition to man to become as an animal *(abêtissez-vous)* is taken literally by Lautréamont.

Maldoror is one of those heroes who, seeing themselves rejected by the world, try to found another kingdom where the language of men will lose its meaning. The act is both defiance and mortification. The theme of expiation is present in *Les Chants,* but it is puzzling because no specific crime has been described. Camus suspects that it might be homosexuality. He finds that Lautréamont's rebel flees to the desert that turns out to be as monotonous and barren as Rimbaud's Harrar. Maldoror tries to extinguish consciousness of his mysterious crime in diverse places such as in the ocean of primitive time, and in diverse ways such as by mingling his voice with the cries of beasts. The rebellion of Maldoror is for Camus another type of conformity.

A few years after *L'homme révolté* of Camus, Aimé Césaire, the poet of Martinique and French senator, wrote, in *Présence Africaine* of 1955, in his *Discours sur le colonialisme,* an interpretation of Lautréamont that seems more penetrating and more just than that of Camus. In his article, Césaire is concerned with an analysis of capitalistic society. He begins an important passage with a quotation: "Everything in this world exudes crime: the newspaper, the wall, the face of man" *(Tout en ce monde sue le crime: le journal, la muraille et le visage de l'homme.)* The author of the sentence is Baudelaire who, Césaire reminds his readers, preceded by many years the advent of Hitler. The Baudelaire quotation was used in order to involve the name of Lautréamont and help dispel the atmosphere of scandal that surrounded *Les Chants de Maldoror* for so long.

Maldoror is the monster, the man of iron, forged by capitalism. Balzac's hero Vautrin was the same type of monster, created in the same way. Maldoror is a Vautrin coming from a warm climate, who wears the wings of an archangel, who suffers mildly from *le paludisme,* and who when he reaches Paris walks along the pavement escorted by Uruguayan vampires. Césaire believes that in time *Les Chants de Maldoror* will be best explained by an historical and sociological interpretation. It is an epic denouncing a precise form of society that existed in Europe, although not always recognized as such, about 1865. When such an interpretation is fully developed, it will be clear that the omnibus episode, for example, is the allegory of a society where a few privileged people are comfortably seated and refuse to make a place for a new arrival. The child in the episode, so harshly rejected, is the proletariat. Baudelaire, in his poem on *Le Chiffonnier* (ragpicker) had given a similar allegory, according to Aimé Césaire. The enemy in *Les Chants,* the anthropophagic creator who is often described in loathsome terms, does not live in the sky. His name can be found in any metropolitan telephone directory. He is probably a member of some board of administrators.

The recent article of Jean-Marie Le Clézio had appeared in *Entretiens* of 1971. At one moment in his career, Le Clézio had planned to write his *thèse de doctorat d'état* on Lautréamont. The article is a summary of very personal observations on the power of *Les Chants.* After a long study of the text, Le Clézio is struck by its mysteriousness, by its impenetrability. It is like a stone *(un caillou)* that all the words of the critics have not dislodged. He calls it the self-sufficient book, an irritant to the reader unable to break it down.

The critics have untiringly tried to make Lautréamont into a "case" study. They have classified him as a writer with themes and a style, with word-frequencies, with a biography and a bibliography, with a morality and a metaphysics. He was one of the inventors of *l'humour noir* and Surrealism. He was perhaps the founder of psychoanalysis. With his use of belladonna, his suffering from schizophrenia, and his possible suicide, Lautréamont was certainly a case for the medical profession.

In this rapid critical review he makes, Le Clézio acknowledges that there is a literary Lautréamont. But he is more concerned with the other Lautréamont who disappeared without leaving any traces. *That* Lautréamont is like an ancient civilization which today is incomprehensible. Our present-day logic is inapplicable to him. That part of Lautréamont's work remains dangerous because like an efficacious poem, it cannot be broken down.

There exists such a perfect cohesion between the man and his work that no explanation was needed, and Lautréamont gave no explanation. He finished his writing and disappeared. A similar cohesion between a life and a lifework is also in Rimbaud. This perfect cohesion places Lautréamont and Rimbaud just outside of literature, in something close to an adventure. Like all adventures, theirs came to an end and left no clues, no significances that an ordinary life would leave.

A further reason for the secretiveness of Lautréamont's work Le Clézio finds in the adolescence of the writing itself. The adolescent world is far more closed than the adult world. Friendless and introverted, Lautréamont played at being a writer as a young boy plays at being a soldier. But such games often reveal terrifying truths.

Le Clézio accumulates evidences in order to point out that we cannot judge Lautréamont with the usual critical criteria. The language of the young when they come under great stress and when they have read omnivorously is indecipherable. Because literature is primarily an ordering of experience, an equilibrium between experience and the expression given to that experience, such writing as that of Rimbaud and Lautréamont will appear subversive, willfully defeating the sense of order that literature by definition seeks to sustain. The shadow of the *lycée* falls over all of Lautréamont's writing, which he dedicates to a few of his schoolmates. Much of the language is incantatory, an evoking of the primitive mysteries: the debauchery of God, the elephant about to die, sexuality, hermaphrodism. In trying to break down the barriers between himself and society, he calls upon the rites, the cries, the gestures of prehistory.

From these brief commentaries, it is evident that serious investigation on Lautréamont has begun. But future critical writings will be far richer than those already published. There is need for a detailed linguistic study of *Les Chants*. A purely psychoanalytical approach to Lautréamont and a purely Marxian approach would illuminate matters that still remain obscure. The relationship between Lautréamont and the entire so-called movement of decadence remains to be done in the domain of literary history. The use of metamorphosis is a central study, in which Lautréamont's use would be contrasted with that of Ovid, Dante, and Kafka. A study should be made of all the possible meanings of the word "God" in *Les Chants de Maldoror*.

CHAPTER 6

Lautréamont and the Movement
of Decadence

I *A Film of 1972*

DURING 1972, a film of Lautréamont was made and shown. Such a hazardous enterprise, under the direction of Michel Butor and Jacques Kupissonof, was destined to have a mixed reception. For those spectators not intimately acquainted with the text of Lautréamont, the film was mysterious and pretentious. For the devoted admirers of the writer, the film failed to realize the beauty and the scope and the importance of the text.

The biographical parts of the film are peaceful transitions between the more violent episodes: scenes of Montevideo, scenes of Paris of the Second Empire based on early documents, façades of the three Paris buildings in which Ducasse lived, letters, and even examination grades from the *lycée* of Tarbes (mediocre grades in literature and excellent grades in mathematics), portraits of writers, Poe, Baudelaire, Hugo, in particular. As parts of the text are read, the film shows appropriate slides, pictures related directly or indirectly to the texts.

In many ways the film was done with intelligence and finesse. It won a prize created by André Malraux: *Prix de la qualité du cinéma français.* Some of the recitation is done by Butor himself. The specific passages chosen to be read illustrate the violence of Lautréamont's imagination, the sumptuousness of his language and rhetoric, and the madness of some of the imagery. Other aspects of the writer's genius and temperament are not well illustrated: Lautréamont the blasphemer, the son of Satan, the revolutionist, the exponent of *l'humour noir,* the poet of night, the initiator of automatic writing.

The Lautréamont exhibited in the film is the writer closest to Byron, Poe, and Hugo. What is missing especially is the writer as adolescent, the student in revolt against the traditional language of professors, the ancestor of Ubu, the literary master of Aragon (at the beginning of Aragon's career) and of Céline, in his repeated attacks against traditional ideas *(idées reçues),* against all the traditional concepts of God and Satan.

So, like the films on Rimbaud, this film on Lautréamont leaves much to be desired. Butor and Kupissonof were well aware of all the difficulties involved and they avoided all the easy processes of vulgarization and pamphleteering. The film is addressed especially to the initiate, and at times the photographic effects are overwhelmingly beautiful, as when the shots of the undersea monsters and strange sea creatures are juxtaposed with the seascapes of horizon and sky.

II *The Meaning of Decadence*

The testament of the nineteenth century, inherited and cherished by the poets of the twentieth century, is best described by the term "spirit of evil." The word is in Baudelaire's title, *Les Fleurs du mal,* and in the phrase devised by Verlaine to designate the new poets: *les poètes maudits.*

The meaning of the word, even more clearly than in *Une saison en enfer* of Rimbaud, is to be deciphered in the apocalyptic images of *Les Chants de Maldoror,* in the tragic horror recorded by that unknown man, le comte de Lautréamont. Even his existence has been doubted by some, and that is in keeping with the kind of revelation made by Lautréamont that transcends literature.

Is it exaggerated to say that the time prophesied by Maldoror has come about? The death of Isidore Ducasse coincided with the fires of the Commune that ravaged the buildings and the streets of Paris in the vicinity of the Bourse. The uprising of the young in Paris, in May, 1968, and the continued contesting of the young during the years that have followed 1968, coincide with the moment in the history of French literature, when the specific testament of Lautréamont seems best to testify to the spirit of evil which the nineteenth century tried to comprehend in the writings of Hugo, Poe, Pétrus Borel, Aloysius Bertrand, Verlaine, Byron, Rimbaud, Huysmans, Baudelaire, of all those associated first with the movement of Les Jeunes-France, and then later with the movement of *les décadents.*

Lucifer is as much a hero as he is the spirit of evil. He was a hero in Tasso's *Gerusalemme liberata,* in Marino's *Strage degli innocenti* and in Milton's *Paradise Lost.* Maldoror is Lucifer fused with the traits of the noble bandit type, destined to perpetrate evil in its extreme forms in order to reveal its power and to find for it names that will be recognized by a contemporary society. "Decadence" is one of those names, which is still in current use, not only as a convenient term, but as a word of reprobation and warning.

Maldoror is Lucifer who appears radiant, powerful, and tormented. In the portrayal of his hero, Lautréamont has mingled ingredients of poetry and delirium, of science and madness. Maldoror is both liberator and a man whose lips are of sulphur. He offers an escape from moral conventions and restrictions, and at the same time he worries his possible neophytes that they are allying themselves with the powers of destruction. Baudelaire had written in his *Journaux intimes* that the perfect type of virile beauty is Satan, in Milton's manner: *le plus parfait type de Beauté virile—à la manière de Milton.*

Satan (or Lucifer) is, after all, the supreme type of outlaw. And the outlaw, no matter how choreographed, no matter how tender or brutal, no matter how attentive or how indifferent, is the Romantic hero. Without having said it as specifically as others, Lautréamont would readily agree that the two guides or sources of inspiration for modern writers were Byron and Sade, the two writers who claimed that the greatest happiness of man is to be found in the committing of crime.

Revolt is the life rhythm of the Romantic. Transgression is just one stage farther along from revolt. *Le bonheur dans le crime* is a title of one of the *Diaboliques* of Barbey d'Aurevilly. Byron required in his heroes a feeling of guilt in order to be aware of any moral sense. Byron was a monster of energy, and Maldoror was a worthy progeny in the sense that passion is the element in which Maldoror lives. In agreement with countless moralists, from Chamfort to Nietzsche, Maldoror would say that the experience of passion gives to a man a higher sense of living, whereas the practice of wisdom gives him merely the sense that he is enduring, that he is continuing to exist. Doesn't Byron compare his blood to the lava boiling "in Aetna's breast of flame"? At Byron's death the scandals reported by journalists were doubtless more excessive than the real events of the poet's life, but they would have been consonant with the life of Maldoror.

As the incarnation of the genius of destruction in the explicit episodes where we see him in action, Maldoror is more profoundly the genius of revolt. The acts themselves are more bloody, more sadistic than the acts of his literary forerunners (except Sade himself), but beyond their literalness, they testify to the need to revolt, the need to clear the way for a renovation, for a spiritual progress. The passionate need for revolt is therefore spiritual, and thus Lautréamont has his place as a forerunner of the boldest thinkers of modern times. To carry out such a mission, he had to denounce the most respectable of sentiments in the name of a higher morality. As Antigone had denounced the laws of the city in the name of the higher laws of God.

It is unjustified to separate the *Poésies* of Lautréamont from *Les Chants*. They are two aspects of the same conviction. *Les Chants* is the revolt against convention, and *Poésies* the revolt against the melancholy, doubt, and despair of Vauvenargues, La Bruyère, and Pascal. In fact, the invective launched against the traditional moralists in *Poésies* is similar to the cries of derision hurled by Maldoror against the Divinity.

The words that come first to our minds as we read *Les Chants:* blasphemy, profanation, sacrilege—are in reality remedies by which Lautréamont is combating injustice. It is as if he were saying that evil has to be exalted first, so that the reign of the good may come about. In the books he has read, Maldoror has not found a reasonable way of separating good from evil, of marking the limits of good and evil. He even raises the question of whether they are the same: evil being the testimonial to man's impotence in reaching the infinite, and the good being the testimonial to man's passion for reaching the infinite. The only sentiment in man that seems real and permanent is the immense sadness he feels as he walks over the face of the earth, as he walks through the labyrinthine streets of the city.

In such settings that are familiar to readers of *Les Chants de Maldoror*, deserted strands of beach, country roads, congested city thoroughfares, parks and brothels, Maldoror appears first, before perpetrating any acts of violence, as an instrument of fate, as a mechanical almost nonhuman being to be utilized by destiny. He comes to life when he begins to react against such a sense of fatality. In destroying the strictures of his fate, he has to, by necessity, destroy the divine power of his fate, and reduce the figure of the Almighty to the figure of a human being.

Everything is presented as enigmatic in the long series of episodes that compose *Les Chants de Maldoror:* dreams, myths, symbols, realistic effects. The son's hostility to the father, or man's effort to liberate himself from his Creator, is the most apparent theme of the work. There are several examples of the traumatic experience of a child being brutally separated from his family: in Canto II, the child running after the omnibus; in Canto IV, the child taking refuge in the ocean and being transformed into an amphibian; and the story of Mervyn in Canto VI.

Literature is primarily a movement of discovery, of self-discovery. In its extreme examples—*Les Chants de Maldoror* is one of these— the discovery of the individual is almost equivalent to the beginning of madness. To know oneself is dangerous, and this danger is emphasized throughout the cantos. The symbolic presentation of the writing, where it is impossible to fix on one meaning alone, where several interpretations occur to the reader, is a way of disguising the danger. The immediate literal interpretation is the shock of melodrama that holds the attention of the reader only momentarily. Then the plethora of possible meanings forms a kind of net in which the reader is caught. He flounders about trying to widen one of the meshes that will permit him to escape.

The libidinous tendencies and the death wish of the subconscious are so numerous and so urgent that the reading of such a work as *Les Chants de Maldoror* provides an almost too exact representation of them. It is difficult to bear the power of the subconscious when it is cast into recognizable forms of violence. Lautréamont is telling us that the individual first recognizes himself as such in his relationship with his father, both his human father and his supernatural Creator. But as soon as this recognition takes place, a combat ensues. A combat for survival which will challenge all the powers of a man. The intense sexual life of an adolescent, as he grows and develops, will constantly recapitulate this combat. Mervyn's story is both his renouncing of his father and his search for a father.

III *Images of the Labyrinth*

Infrequently Lautréamont alludes to the strong words of "Minotaur" and "labyrinth," associated not only with Greek mythology, but also with the writings of Sade, and which are striking symbols for Lautréamont's conception of the life of every individual. Life is not static. It is constantly moving, both progressing and retrogressing. It is constantly moving into danger and out of danger.

In his subconscious man creates his own labyrinth, and then in his conscious life he tries to explore it and understand it. Each man therefore plays the two roles of Minotaur, of monster for whom the labyrinth is designed, and the heroic role of Theseus who tries to encounter the Minotaur and slay him. What is usually called "conflict" or "plot" or "action" in a play or a novel, is the meeting between Theseus and the Minotaur, between the conscious and the subconscious life of a man. Maldoror, even in the resonance of his name, is the Minotaur, and at times, in his more rational states, he is Theseus. The cantos are the labyrinth, comparable to the circles of Dante's *Inferno*. They are, in both works, the literary expression of man seen in his labyrinthine ways.

As a writer, Lautréamont is totally conscious in his labors of reconstructing the labyrinth, classically logical in the ordering of his sentences and in their transitions. But behind these formal aspects, he is searching for the obscure forces of a psyche, searching in his movements toward the future and toward the past for the meaning of the drives and the emotions of a man's life.

The danger of such an exploration is that of losing one's way, of coming upon complete alienation from one's conscious life. But in the labyrinth of *Les Chants,* in each phase of the search, the hero finds his way, even if it is momentarily, as in the popular horror melodrama story of the *série noire* type: Fantômas, for example, or James Bond. When Lautréamont speaks directly to the reader about his work, he emphasizes his logic and his prudence in the way in which he reveals the unusual and the fantastic. In order to approximate the great reason for life, he procedes reasonably.

It is indeed reasonable to look upon sleep and nightmares as experiences that reveal the life and the drives of the subconscious. Sleep, madness, and death are states where the deepest ego comes to life. A conscious effort to see clearly into oneself is quite different from the vision provided by the subconscious. Lautréamont is both analyst and psychoanalyst: analyst in the lucidity of his form, and psychoanalyst in the obscurities of his form's meaning.

The writer is always to some degree the recreator of myths. The defiance of Maldoror is of such proportions, the violence of his actions and his thoughts is so extreme that he becomes the personification of evil, an evil figure in the very greatness of that which he opposes.

The psychoanalysis of a character reveals what Maldoror reveals in a literary form: the close relationship existing between the subconscious and the symbol. The labyrinth and the desert can easily symbolize the subconscious: the one compared to too many paths, and the other, pathless. From Greece and from Egypt come the two myths of the Minotaur and the Sphinx, two figures who complement one another: the Minotaur with the animal head and the human body, the Sphinx with the female head and the animal's body.

Maldoror encounters the Minotaur in the episodes of bestiality, and the Sphinx in the efforts to explain the enigmas of existence. The supernatural powers he manifests, the swiftness of his movements, his ubiquity, make him appear as an archangel hesitating between good and evil, fearful of God and wanting to be God. He thus traces the limitations that both separate good from evil and that unite them.

In the books he has read, Maldoror-Lautréamont has found no answers to his questions. He scorns all reading and vilifies the authors. When he equates evil with good, as a possible hypothesis for an understanding of the behavior of men, he is very close to the philosophy of Sade. Without always naming the extremes, heaven and hell, Maldoror, like some winged creature from both realms, moves between them, and maintains the traditional connotations of heaven as being a very lofty region of serenity, and hell as being a dizzying abyss of evil.

All conformity is a source of loathing for Lautréamont. The artist, more than most men, is opposed to all forms of submission that might represent an acceptance of conformity. Poetry loses out when it fails to startle or shock its readers. Poetry can have nothing to do with the political events of society. It must remain in regions that are above politics, in regions that are comparable to the vastness of the ocean from which the poet may draw freshness of inspiration, and a vision that has nothing to do with the smallness of man's daily avarice and egoism.

IV *Decadence and Violence*

The earliest of the serious interpreters of Lautréamont—Gaston Bachelard, for example, and Léon Pierre-Quint—did not point out the likely inspiration of a book which Lautréamont undoubtedly knew: *Frankenstein* by Mary Shelley. In this Gothic novel, the monster created by Frankenstein hurls at his creator reproaches that are similar to the reproaches spoken to God by Maldoror. Frankenstein himself has to turn away from the monster he created through a feeling of disgust for him. Both the monster and Maldoror curse their creator and are cursed by him.

The appetite for destruction in Maldoror is never satisfied. Like the sexual needs of man, there is no hint of compromise or satisfaction in Maldoror's urge to destroy. He closes himself off from suffering in his will to impose suffering on others. The monstrousness of his deeds contrasts with the beauty of his appearance. In the ultimate episode of *Les Chants,* the story of Mervyn serves to point up the dual power of beauty. The adolescent beauty of Mervyn is such that it must be destroyed. It is too extreme for nature to tolerate. Society, which is nature provided with means to annihilate whatever is exceptional, cannot allow the extreme—beauty or genius—to exist for long. And then, the more mature and more mysterious beauty of Maldoror—like that of Milton's Lucifer—is the disguise which permits him to carry out the destruction. If Maldoror had not been strikingly handsome, Mervyn would not have followed him.

The Luciferian power of metamorphosis is in Maldoror, as it is in the paintings of Cranach and Hieronymus Bosch, and in the writings of Ovid and Dante and Kafka. Maldoror's copulation with the shark exemplifies his power to move beyond the humiliations of conventional form. In the chaos of destruction there is always the chance for a new birth. A new form may rise up from the wasteland, from the battlefield, from the earthquake, from the volcanic eruption that destroys a town. The earliest forms of nature obsess the mind of Lautréamont: *la poulpe* (octopus), *la sangsue* (bloodsucker), *le requin* (shark), *l'hermaphrodite, le pou* (louse), *le cheveu de Dieu* (the hair of God).

Scenes of the creation and apocalyptic scenes are fused in these visions, where the themes of destruction and rebirth are also fused. The form of Maldoror in his spectacular beauty, and in his ubiquity, presides over the forces of death and birth. He is responsible for both: for the scenes of Genesis and the scenes of Revelation. The way is opened up to the richness of form which the movements of Cubism and Surrealism will provide.

The world is so mistreated by Maldoror, so manipulated, so pulverized that *Les Chants* appears as a work in competition with Genesis. It is a new beginning of forms that have attracted artists since its time. The poet and the painter have been encouraged by the example of his work to create their forms in a greater sense of freedom, and especially, with greater boldness. New readers of Lautréamont in the 1970's find the book to be "far out," or "out of sight," if we use the current phrases of approval spoken by the young. Maldoror, the new archangel of our age, is still obliterating traces of the older Classicism and guiding the acts of the youngest rebels.

The rich and very complex interrelationships between "Decadence" and "violence" account for the ever increasing importance and popularity of Lautréamont. The terms themselves have as many connotations as "Romanticism" and "Realism" because they are capable of as many changes as society itself and the fashions of society. "Dandy" is another term closely related to "Romantic" and "Decadent" which began in England with Beau Brummel and Byron, but which flourished especially in France with Musset first and then with Baudelaire who rebaptized the word and gave it a strongly spiritual meaning.

With Maldoror the dandy became satanic and seraphic. Maldoror combines the Byronic dandy, the figure of a Dante after he has completed his voyage through hell, the decadent Des Esseintes who has experienced all the sensuous perversions, and the face of the rebel of all centuries including *l'homme révolté* of Albert Camus in the early 1950's, and Alex in *A Clockwork Orange,* Kubrick's film of the early 1970's.

From such a list of names, writers and heroes both, it is not difficult to see that their abiding trait is diabolical. Lucifer was archangel and traitor. He was both pure spirit, ubiquitous in his power of flight, and eager in his pride to know all the experiences of man's sensuous nature even if that meant renouncing the highest place among God's angels. He was paradoxical as every man who follows him is paradoxical: pure in spirit and good in heart because of his original closeness to God; and yet attracted to rebellion in order to indulge his overwhelming pride; and driven to know all the sensuality of his nature, the elegances of the dandy, all the multiple variations of sexual experience, the experiments of deca-

dent taste. Lucifer has countless names because he exists in disguise—
he is the supreme literary hero who combines legend with history:
Nero, Gilles de Rais, Petronius, Alcibiades, Blake, Baudelaire,
Pétrus Borel, Sade, Hoffmann, Poe, Rimbaud, Maldoror of
Lautréamont, and Alex of *A Clockwork orange.*

We have just named a triad of motivations or impulses: spirituality, rebellion, and sensuality—and we have associated them
first with the fallen archangel Lucifer, and then with artists, and
finally with heroes created by artists. Would it not be more accurate
to say that this triune activity or fantasy is in every man, and is
merely given its clearest delineation by the artist in the projection
of his hero?

The young artists of the nineteenth century talked against the
bourgeois spirit, as the young artists today speak against the Establishment. The bourgeoise and the Establishment are terms glorify-
ing health, security, success, common sense, the household. But the
young in heart see in such a society factories that make guns and
democracies that are built on the misuse of money. It is because of
their deep spirituality that the young protest against the tyranny of
a philistine epoch.

The bourgeoisie in power, whether it be the France of Louis-
Philippe, or the United States of Nixon, will look upon the rebellious
young as dilettanti of corrupting sins, as lovers of orgies, as vision-
aries of dreams and "trips." Whatever appears to the young as a
force of liberation and vision, will be named by those in power as
unhealthy, immoral, and unpatriotic. Whereas the ordinary youth
will try to argue with the older established generation and plead his
position, the hero, or the dandy, or the Maldoror figure who has
reached heroic proportions, will not argue. To be misunderstood is
part of his glory. In his rebellion he appears as the spiritual aristocrat
who feels himself superior to the average man.

V *The Dandy*

Baudelaire's dandy is remembered especially for his attempts
"to astonish *(épater)* the bourgeois," but he was in reality more
concerned with affirming his right to create an aristocratic art that
would delight a minority. Des Esseintes in *A rebours* of Huysmans
was the so-called "decadent" hero, who was pleased when the phi-

listines of his society attacked him for sins he did not commit. He encouraged all the legends about him. They protected him and made him seem more distant from the ordinary man than he actually was. The attitude of the dandy and the decadent was for the most part a pose, a disguise that would make him appear as an idler, a dreamer, a sensualist. Behind that pose of seeming indolence, he was in reality a hard-working writer, involved in periodicals, publishing houses, exhibitions, manifestos, waging war on his opponents.

The dandy's languor and his antics were always taken too seriously. And in the same way, the extreme acts of violence in such a work as *Les Chants de Maldoror* are taken too literally. Of course, the distance between eccentricities and acts of sadism is very great. But so is the distance between an aesthete and an archangel. It is the distance between a critical reproach and anathema. Baudelaire as dandy, Des Esseintes as decadent, and Maldoror as perpetrator of evil acts, lend themselves too easily to the role of scapegoat. But that is what they become when their dandyism, their decadence, and their evil are clearly delineated in the art of literature. It is easy for readers to forget that literature is greater than life, greater in the sense that it is more explicit, aggrandized, blown up to such a degree that facial traits and temperamental traits are seen for the first time.

The reasons for a young man appearing as a poseur in real life are more significant than the various poses he has appropriated in each generation: a *petit maître* at the time of Molière, a pale Werther in the eighteenth century, a Jeune-France in the 1830's, a dandy in the 1850's, a decadent in the 1880's, a dadaist in the 1920's, an angry young man in the 1950's, a hippie in the 1960's, a freak in the 1970's. Every age and every country has its Greenwich Village and its *Village Voice*. But when such a voice is recorded by such a writer as Lautréamont, the very act of recording it makes the voice more strident and more articulate than it was in real life. The pose is eliminated, and the real figure is projected from the fantasy-life of the writer.

The dandy-writer in the nineteenth century, Baudelaire and Théophile Gautier, for example, as they appeared in cafés and salons, and the more sequestered youth in his Paris hotel room, Rimbaud and Ducasse, were inevitably described by the journalists of their age as anemic and degenerate. They were compared to a royal race of men at the end of a dynasty, diseased with the maladies that corrupted Rome, physiologically exhausted. There was no one in Paris in

1869–1870 to write about Ducasse, as Gautier had written about Baudelaire, and Verlaine had written about Rimbaud. But these friends, "le bon Théophile" and "le pauvre Lélian," had helped to create and disseminate the very legends about Baudelaire and Rimbaud that convinced the ordinary citizens of the iniquities of all art and the diabolic traits characterizing all artists.

The legends that might have made him into le comte de Lautréamont are the cantos of Maldoror. His texts contain all the proof needed to make Ducasse appear as the setting sun of an aged civilization (the image used by Baudelaire to describe decadence). The texts are rehearsals of neuroses and of passions grown depraved, of obsessions that turn a man to madness.

Baudelaire had died just prior to the Franco-Prussian War, and Lautréamont wrote his work during the war. When it was over, the defeat of France at the hands of the new German Empire was explained by the theory that the Latin races had fallen into a final decadence. Two lines of Verlaine were interpreted as describing the fall of the French Empire and the appearance of the German soldiers:

> *Je suis l'Empire à la fin de la Décadence,*
> *Et vois passer les grands barbares blancs.*

When the little magazine *Le Décadent* began appearing in the 1880's, it did not represent a decadent program. It was intended to be an insult to the established literature. But the title was seized upon by the journalists and applied to everything in French letters that seemed languid and aesthetic and immoral. It was used indiscriminately to describe the Realistic novels of the Goncourt brothers, the Symbolist novels of Huysmans, the musical Impressionist verse of Verlaine, the stronger more Classical poetry of Baudelaire, the ironical poems of Laforgue, the difficult poems of Mallarmé. In a word, decadent was a synonym of the modern poet who was classified as half-mad and half-degenerate. The general judgment was ludicrously severe: the French race and all the traditions of the Republic were being threatened by the modern writer.

For Rousseau, decadence begins whenever the natural simplicity of man is changed by the intrusion of any form of artificial civilization. But for the anti-Rousseauist, decadence begins whenever primitive elements appear in the art or the morals of a civilization. Since the time of Lautréamont, decadence is attached especially to the concept of individualism, to the type of man who seems unadaptable to social obligations.

Maldoror is seen to be the enemy of society. His speech as well as his actions are individualistic. Opponents of Modernism have always sought for signs of decadence in the very style and syntax of the new writers. But almost always, as in the case of Lautréamont, they confuse the content of the work with the style of the writing. The sentences of Lautréamont are as unified and clear as those of Baudelaire, and yet both were classified by their early opponents as decadents, enemies of the moral health of the nation.

Verlaine, when questioned about the word "decadence," insisted that it meant nothing in particular, that it was being used as a war cry or as an insult. The founder of the magazine *Le Décadent,* A. Baju, gave it a positive meaning. A *décadent* for him was a skeptic and therefore a believer in the progress of civilization. Is there a workable definition of decadence somewhere between these two extreme definitions? Much of the confusion comes from the determination of most critics to associate closely a decadence in art with a decadence in morals.

The simplest definition of decadent is the type of writer following in time a master and who by comparison with the strength of the master seems weak and imitative. Shakespeare, Racine and Baudelaire, to choose three powerful writers, did have imitators following them whose art lacks the strength and the innovative vitality of the masters. In this restricted sense, they can be looked upon as decadent writers whose work appears weak or even incomprehensible. But to call their work "degenerate" is to confuse art with morality.

The case of Lautréamont is different. He certainly had ancestors among the writers of Gothic tales, but his work today seems more innovative than theirs, stronger than theirs, and one that continues to have a greater impact on the new readers of succeeding generations. Lautréamont was a new beginning in literature. In the domain of literary violence, *Les Chants* holds a position similar to that held by *A rebours* of Huysmans in the domain of literary aestheticism. Both works, the epic story of Maldoror and the sensational experiences of Des Esseintes, after serving as signs of degeneracy for decades, now seem to be signs of pure revolt; not aberrations, but vigorous renewals of strength.

Fifty years after Lautréamont's death, the Surrealists were sensitive to his power and proclaimed his importance to an unbelieving world. But the Surrealists formed a small world in the 1920's. It has taken one hundred years for a public to evolve, a youthful public in particular, that can find in *Les Chants de Maldoror* the reflections of its own fantasy world, and a public willing to acknowledge such a discovery. For a century, *Les Chants* has been a work in search of its public. During this same time, approximately, *A rebours* has had a small but fervent public in each generation. It seems destined to be limited to that kind of public, because of its overrefinement, because of the impression it gives of being a case history in aestheticism. It is more purely a work of art, a treatise on extravagant aesthetics, an apology for a way of living. *Les Chants* has at its center the expression of a will to destroy by violence and vituperation what is impeding man in his self-exploration.

VI *Maldoror and Other Heroes*

In the same way that Petronius has come to life for today's generation in Fellini's film on *The Satyricon,* so Lautréamont appears more logical and more comprehensible in the new film of violence, at the head of which one is inclined to place *A Clockwork Orange.* Alex preys on individuals in his society, as Maldoror does in his society, and in each case, society is ill defined in any historical sense. It is recognizable as society, but it is no one historical society. It is the society we recognize more clearly as being that of our dreams and our fantasies, where we see ourselves both victimized and triumphant where all of our mild daily conflicts reappear heightened and dramatized in orgiastic color and movement.

Whereas the young generation reading *Maldoror* and viewing *Clockwork* are impressed by the structure of the works, the mathematical precision and neatness of the performances, the unfolding and the sequence of the scenes, the older generation of readers and spectators tend to close the book or leave the theater because they follow the literalness of the action and are disarmed or disgusted by such literalness. Because of their age, the young are able to move easily from the realism of violence in life and art to its relationship with their fantasy-life. The child is not as upset by violence as the adult is. And likewise, the late adolescent, the student in our universities today, imposes on the endless pictures of violence perpetrated daily in every country he reads of, the related pictures of his dreams and fantasies.

The memorable episodes of *Maldoror:* the brothel, the omnibus, the shark, the bulldog, Mervyn, are comparable to scenes in *Clockwork*—the milk bar, the drugstore scene, the parental apartment, the gang-rape—and they are all recognizable as elements in our contemporary world. But the atmosphere of every scene in both works has elements of fantasy, and especially of phallic fantasy. The opening shot in the film, the close-up of Alex' face where we see especially the false eyelashes on an eye, is reminiscent of the passages in Lautréamont where the lips of Maldoror are described, the jasper, the sapphire lips. One detail of the face represents the hero. It is exaggerated melodramatically to encourage the audience to accept the hero in his monstrousness. The eyes and the lips of these heroes are facile symbols for the power—the almost diabolical power—they exercise over others.

No film comes closer than *Clockwork* to revealing both graphically and dramatically the youth culture today, and no literary work comes closer than *Maldoror* to revealing the ease with which today's youth culture fuses realism with fantasy. To the obvious themes of violence, drugs and eroticism, one should add, in order to account for the second part of the film, and to understand the conclusion of each canto, the philosophical theme of pessimism. *A Clockwork Orange* seems the most pessimistic work of art since the days of Dada. And since Dadaism demeaned or refused the production of art, we might claim *Clockwork* in its absolute pessimism of 1972 the equal of *Les Chants de Maldoror* of 1870. This means that a century has been framed by two works equal in their graphic power: one in words and one in pictures, and equal in their revolt against society.

In both *Clockwork* and *Maldoror,* the violence is so highly stylized that the time of the action is not quite the present. Is it tomorrow or the day after tomorrow? At least we are made to have the uneasy feeling that it is closer than we think. Malcolm McDowell seems to be the star of the future, the ultimate teen-ager whom we fear and whom we are drawn to. The teen-age bar that legally dispenses drug-spiked milk indicates at the beginning that we are not exactly in the present, but such a bar is predictably not very far off. There is a similar timelessness in *Les Chants de Maldoror,* in most Gothic tales, and in the marquis de Sade.

The very names Des Esseintes and Maldoror, in their suggested etymology, *essences* and *saints* in Des Esseintes, and *mal d'aurore* in the Lautréamont name, point out the quests of the two heroes: the mystical quest in Huysmans, and the pursuit of evil in Lautréamont. By establishing "correspondences," Des Esseintes experiments with all his senses: olfactory, visual, auditive, and these experiments, both ingenuous and complicated, are not unlike the acts of violence by which Maldoror tests his aptitude for change and revolt. Overtones of satire in both works keep the reader from losing himself literally in the narratives. Parody softens realism. It is there to remind us that man's hatred for society is also his love for society.

VII *Baudelaire and Lautréamont*

Both Des Esseintes and Maldoror lived a secluded life. And so when they actually participate in a scene from life, it resembles an hallucination. In the prose poems of Baudelaire, greatly admired by Des Esseintes, we have scenes of Paris where the supernatural spirit of evil has totally captured the realistic traits and transformed them into a dream sequence. The poets of 1885 had turned Baudelaire into the poet they desired. At that time they had little need for Lautréamont. The separate pieces of *Les Fleurs du mal* and *Spleen de Paris* were strong enough for them. It would have been hard for them to assimilate the continuous actions of the epic-like hero Maldoror.

Baudelaire's poem *Les sept vieillards* gives an eerie picture of Paris and an eerie quality to the poet's experience of observing an old man stumbling through mud and snow. When the poet sees not one but *seven* of these figures, he takes flight and describes his soul dancing like an old boat (*une gabarre*) mastless on a monstrous sea. Baudelaire's vision is multiplied seven times and the vision is as horrifying as anything in Lautréamont. What Baudelaire evokes is evil. It is not imaginary, it is real and has to be translated into comprehensible language. This is the process called by Baudelaire *sorcellerie évocatoire*, which he follows. The symbol in Baudelaire or the vision in Lautréamont is used in order for the writer to reach a more accurate understanding.

Ten years before Lautréamont wrote *Maldoror*, Baudelaire wrote his poem *Hymne à la Beauté* (1860) in which Baudelaire asks Beauty (addressed as if she were a woman) whether she was from hell or from heaven:

> *Viens-tu du ciel profond ou sors-tu de l'abîme,*
> *O Beauté?*

In the list of jewels worn by Beauty, "horror" is one of the most charming. "Murder" is a trinket dancing on her belly. Because Beauty dispenses both joy and sorrow, we could ask whether Baudelaire's figure is not Fortune of the Middle Ages, the blind goddess who controls the fate of every man. Such essential ambiguity as we see in *Hymne à la Beauté* is everywhere in *Les Chants de Maldoror.* The infernal, the fatal, the irresponsible seem to be our legacies, which we drink as a *philtre,* as some magic potion that inspires love or hate or the desire to destroy. Baudelaire asks whether Beauty is a blessing or a curse:

De Satan ou de Dieu, qu'importe? Ange ou Sirène? and the same question is asked by Lautréamont when he substitutes *Life* for *Beauty.* If modern beauty must have something ironic about it, the very word itself "ironic" seems to involve the diabolical.

Baudelaire and Lautréamont were individual artists in their own right, but they were also the trend of an entire literature. The "shadow of the Divine Marquis," as Mario Praz characterizes the influence of Sade in his *Romantic Agony,* fell on almost everyone in the nineteenth century: Chateaubriand as well as M. G. Lewis, on Hoffmann as well as Hugo and Sand, on Shelley as well as Maturin and Pétrus Borel. Even Berlioz, in his opera *Harold en Italie,* stressed the macabre and the blasphemous. Musset's *Confession d'un enfant du siècle* (1836) is not heeded very much today, and that is probably because it is no longer widely read. Its character, Octave, demonstrates practices of a libertine and actions that are sadistically cruel.

When Baudelaire describes the effect of Delacroix's paintings, he uses the term "lake of blood haunted by wicked angels" *(lac de sang hanté de mauvais anges).* Delacroix often chose scenes of slaughter and rape for his pictures, Baudelaire found them to be allied with a sense of "irremediable suffering" that characterized Delacroix himself. The concubines, murdered on the funeral bed of Sardanapalus, is one example of the vivid sensuality in the paintings.

It is customary today to admire the Baudelaire poems that seem the most universal: *Le Voyage, Le Cygne, Recueillement, L'Amour du mensonge,* and to neglect or avoid those pieces that impressed the most deeply the generation of Lautréamont: *Les Femmes damnées, La Charogne, Une Martyre.*

One of the effects of today's renewed interest in Lautréamont is a reexamination of the satanic poems of Baudelaire that deal directly with the force of evil, sadism, debauchery. Baudelaire's own claim to originality was his attempt to extract beauty from evil, and this he called, somewhat erroneously, an unexplored domain. Actually, Baudelaire invented no new horrors. And neither did Lautréamont. But both revived the theme of the macabre and gave it a new literary value and form. Baudelaire was probably more affected and more deliberately the mystifier than Lautréamont. But it is not difficult to see in both Baudelaire and Lautréamont characteristics of reticence and even shyness which forced them to create extreme blatant and colorful scenes, and metaphors that screen and protect their native shyness. Any other kind of expression given to their experiences might have seemed ineffectual and pallid. In the hands of an artist, a mere device may become an art form in itself.

When Baudelaire spoke of cultivating his hysteria *(j'ai cultivé mon hystérie),* he described what happens whenever the artist is immersed in his work. The act of writing brings to the surface what is not usually seen in a human being. The extreme episodes in Lautréamont do not correspond to what he was in his daily life. No traits of Maldoror could be seen in the face or the behavior of Isidore Ducasse. The unexpected impulses to violence, the seemingly unmotivated drive to commit an evil action, the pattern of fantasy that comes from a part of a man's psyche that is unfamiliar to himself— these are commented on directly in *Spleen de Paris* and used in the unfolding of the brief tales. There is a similar air of wonderment in Lautréamont as Maldoror obeys impulses of cruelty and perpetuates sadistic acts that normally would place him in the prison of any land.

Whereas the judges and most members of society call such impulses and such acts perverse, Baudelaire and Lautréamont make every effort to induce their readers to see them as primal drives of the human heart, as impulses which, with other impulses, constitute the character of a man. To be told that one must abstain from committing such and such an act, is equivalent to instituting a desire to commit the act. The subconscious becomes the receptacle of acts which the conscious self of a man will not commit. They are committed then in his fantasy life. . . or in his literary works. There, in the unmistakable clarity of a written page, a canto of Dante or of Lautréamont, a prose poem of Baudelaire or Rimbaud, the evidence is made clear, revealing the dual force of good and evil, of love and hate that inhabits us simultaneously.

The reader, mysteriously drawn to Lautréamont, discovers there subjects of his own dreams and nightmares, acts never actually committed by him, but recognized by him. Baudelaire, when he first came upon the writings of Edgar Allen Poe, claims that he saw there sentences and thoughts written down by himself twenty years earlier. In his analysis of Poe's story *Ligeia,* D. H. Lawrence *(Studies in Classic American Literature)* speaks of that drive in a man to know a woman too well, to love her too deeply. Such a longing, such a love, is a form of vampirism. Love is, in fact, treated at times as vampirism in Poe, Baudelaire, and Lautréamont. Ecstasy easily turns into an obsession, which in its turn becomes destructive and annihilating.

The passage in Canto II of *Les Chants,* where Maldoror and God are called two neighboring monarchs *(deux monarques voisins)* in even rivalry one with the other, is in agreement with countless passages in Sade and in a few critical passages in Baudelaire, where a sinful state is looked upon as the normal state of man's nature.

Maldoror is natural man, as opposed to the general conception of morality in the eighteenth century. For Lautréamont, as well as for his leading predecessors Sade and Baudelaire, nature is not the source of the good and the beautiful. Nature itself is at the source of what society and the Church call crime: the killing of another human being, the impulse to sequester and torture and even devour. Parricide and anthropophagy are counseled by nature.

Woman, in her naturalness, is described as the perpetrator of abominations by Sade (in *Juliette*), by Baudelaire (in *Bénédiction*) and by Lautréamont (in Canto IV:3, where the mother and wife torture their son and husband). The peremptory sentence in Baudelaire's *Journaux intimes* is a distillation of this misogynist view: *La femme est "naturelle," c'est-à-dire abominable.* In the same work, Baudelaire establishes an equivalence between cruelty and voluptuousness by calling them identical sensations. *Cruauté et volupté, sensations identiques.*

The Mervyn-Maldoror episode in Canto VI could easily be interpreted as an illustration of Baudelaire's theory of love where each of the partners in love, when he or she is being drawn to the other, inevitably plays one of two roles: victim and executioner. One partner will find in passivity and masochism a voluptuousness which the other partner will discover in the experience of domination and sadism.

The audible expression given to suffering in sexual love changes quickly to pleasure, as the ferociousness of the male attack shifts to the ecstatic pleasure of conquest. In any extreme experience of the senses, such as the climactic point of sexual love, the nature of both man and woman is changed into a force that is almost unrecognizable.

Dante, in order to permit his reader to understand this experience of sexual love, uses the image of violent gusts of wind within which the lovers have no control over themselves. Baudelaire uses in *Duellum* the image of two armed warriors fighting to the death. All six cantos of *Maldoror* represent Lautréamont's hero as tracking his victims in episode after episode, until he finds one he can really love, and then he sets about deliberately and methodically to destroy the victim-lover so that no infidelity can ever be perpetrated by the victim.

Such is the drive in man to find fulfillment in love that all forms and alternatives are open to him. The literary artist has within his capacity, within his craft, the most violent and the most hyperbolic acts to call upon and to exploit, as if the experience of reading such scenes will be substituted by the reader for such actions in his own life. Maldoror's sexual union with the shark comes early in the book (Canto II:13). Between that scene, which has its own quality of shock and monstrousness, and the Mervyn murder in Canto VI, where the love object is an adolescent boy, we have moved to a scene that combines sadism with decadence in a moral sense.

To believe one's lover a monstrous creature seems to be a characteristic of sadism. Several poems of Baudelaire attest to this (*Tu mettrais l'univers* and *Le vampire,* for example), and in his prose writing Baudelaire often argues with himself and with his reader about the natural drive in man to look for *une femme vicieuse* as a partner in love. The horrible is able to stimulate the experience of ardor in man. The limitless reserves of energy in Maldoror are stirred by pictures of possible conquest that in most cases are characterized by monstrousness.

The title of Baudelaire's prose poem *Mademoiselle Bistouri* resembles the typical title of pornographic books on sale today in specialized bookshops. But Baudelaire's use of the macabre in so many of his best poems and prose poems, is never unaccompanied by his persistent effort to comprehend such attraction in himself and in other men, and his deep-seated sympathy for the suffering and the dramas that arise out of such drives. Lautréamont is more melodramatic and more ruthless than Baudelaire in his depiction of such scenes. At no point does his sympathy for human plight reach the poignancy of Baudelaire's. He of course was younger and far less experienced than Baudelaire. But that very recklessness of the young allows us to see in Lautréamont more clearly than in the writings of Baudelaire, the extremes of human repressions. His fantasies are more obsessional, more bare, and more visible than those of Baudelaire.

Taken together, the Baudelaire poems and the Lautréamont cantos prepared the way for the *fin-de-siècle* books, beginning with *A rebours,* where the artifices and refinement of the so-called decadent spirit are exhibited. Baudelaire's exceptional sensitivity to the sadistic and masochistic impulses of man's nature, and his determination at least to record them even if he could not always explain them scientifically, needed as illustrations those pictures of pure violence and psychic upheaval we read in Lautréamont. Each needed the other: Baudelaire the philosopher of evil and Lautréamont the exponent of evil. The writers who followed them, Huysmans and Oscar Wilde and Hugo von Hoffmanstahl, for example, describe in their books the quests for the sensational and the putrescent. Stronger writers who performed after the 80's and 90's, those decades so marked by Baudelaire, assimilated the more purely decadent traits of those decades, and brought them into play with the more life-redeeming motifs that characterize the universal literature of the masters: Dante, Shakespeare, Milton, Racine, Goethe.

The new literary masters of the twentieth century, Gide, Proust, Joyce, Mann, Kafka, have drawn heavily on specifically decadent traits which the literary tradition in France associates with Baudelaire and Lautréamont. The scenes and episodes in the books of the new masters, which are already classical and classified, are more richly orchestrated and transpire in more recognizable settings than the scenes in *Les Chants:* Marcel's sequestering Albertine in his parents' apartment in Paris and submitting her, his captive, to the daily torture of interrogation; Aschenbach stalking Tadzio in the streets of Venice, in a pattern not unlike that of Maldoror's pursuit of Mervyn; Leopold Bloom's walk through Dublin as he thinks of his dead son, and as he unconsciously pursues Stephen, his spiritual son; Michel of *L'Im-*

moraliste, forcing his wife Marceline to move ever farther south in Algeria and thus bring about her certain death.

The themes of violence and esoterism have joined during the past one hundred years, and helped to create a literary art often referred to as "decadent." Readers today recognize themselves in it, although it might not be difficult to prove that literature has exerted its own forcefulness in fashioning and forming modern man. Is it true that nature imitates art, as Oscar Wilde claimed? Baudelaire's evocative witchcraft *(sorcellerie évocatoire)* and Rimbaud's verbal alchemy *(alchimie du verbe)* are experiments which, when taken with Lautréamont's apostrophes to God, account for the development of an entire aspect of modern literature which in very recent years has been made visibly real in such films as *Rosemary's Baby, Satyricon,* and *A Clockwork Orange.*

The resurgent interest in Balzac in the past thirty years is due not to *Eugénie Grandet* as much as to *Seraphita* and *Louis Lambert* and *La Recherche de l'absolu.* The specific lessons on the occult provided by a Mme Blavatsky seem unnecessary since the writings of W. B. Yeats and such a work as *Arcane 17* of André Breton, and prior to them, *Les Chimères* of Nerval. The literary movement of Symbolism reestablished the study of the occult in order to offset or counterbalance the intense development of science. The newest studies on Rabelais and Maurice Scève seem to emphasize the tradition of the occult which their writings incorporate.

The study of magic and alchemy are not unrelated to the experiments of self-induced sleep practiced by some of the Surrealists. Astrology, as studied and practiced by Max Jacob in Montmartre and by Léon-Paul Fargue in the Saint-Germain neighborhood of Paris, and more recently by Henry Miller in Big Sur, California, represents an effort of the literary artist to break through locked labyrinthine ways of man's psychic life. Rather than describing the sensations stimulated by his experiences, Lautréamont was more concerned with a search for the keys with which to unlock the mysteries of the psyche.

Ever since the hermetic sonnets of Nerval, and such a poem as *Prose pour Des Esseintes* of Mallarmé, the poetic act has been interpreted in its relationship with magic as well as in its more traditional relationship with religious and metaphysical ambitions. In André Breton's novel *Nadja,* there is a spiritualist *(une voyante)* who plays a part as important as that of the clairvoyante Mme Sosostris in Eliot's *Wasteland*.

Between the period when Delacroix was producing his greatest paintings, and the Symbolist moment when Gustave Moreau was completing those paintings of his that seemed to illustrate the sensitivity of the *fin-de-siècle,* there evolved the nineteenth-century conception of the Fatal Man and the Fatal Woman in which Lautréamont's Maldoror occupies a central position.

VIII *Flaubert and Lautréamont*

Emma Bovary as *femme fatale* preceded Maldoror as *homme fatal* by just a few years. In the novel itself, there are various clues to Flaubert's interest in Sade, and even his obsession with Sade. The Goncourts in their *Journal* never failed to report on what they considered, perhaps unjustly, as this obsession of Flaubert's mind. But when Emma herself chooses books that might have been those of Sade, *tableaux orgiaques* and *situations sanglantes* are words in the text that describe those scenes which affect Emma. In *Salammbô* there is a scene where a handsome male slave is tortured before his beloved goddess. When as a young boy in *La Légende de Saint Julien l'hospitalier,* Julien strangles a pigeon, he almost faints from the savage pleasure he experiences as his hand feels the dying convulsions of the bird. Scene after scene in *La Tentation de Saint Antoine* is comparable to a sadistic orgy. Slaughter, blood, flagellations are commonplaces in the narrative. As in Lautréamont, scenes of cruelty in Flaubert are usually accompanied by profanation. The sacrilegious seems inevitably to be a part of the obscene.

The taste for the violent and the sadistic in many of the arch-Romantics, and not only in Flaubert, is continued in Lautréamont, in Barbey d'Aurevilly *(Diaboliques)* in Pétrus Borel *(Rhapsodes),* and perhaps especially in Théophile Gautier *(Mademoiselle de Maupin).* The character d'Albert, in his letters, in the Gautier novel, analyses at length his fantasies which concern the impossible kind of life he would like to know. The kind of life he actually leads holds no attraction for him. He cherishes the dreams he has of such characters as Tiberius, Caligula and Nero, the great Romans of the Empire, those who had been able to extirpate from themselves any sense of pity for mankind.

D'Albert, in his wildest fantasies, would go far beyond the actions and perversions of a Heliogabolis. His circuses would be more bloody than those of the Roman emperor, his slaves more numerous and more handsome. He dreamed of new towers of Babel that would reach the sky and from which he could spit down on all of creation. Since he can't be a man in the normal sense, why can't he be God? Such cries and such fantasies are precisely those of Maldoror, written down in the following generation.

In *Mademoiselle de Maupin* and throughout the writings of Flaubert, the figure of Nero is often invoked as the culminating figure of Antiquity. The emperor had been venerated in the same way by Sade in *Juliette: O Néron, laisse-moi vénérer ta mémoire.* The hero of Flaubert's early novel *Novembre* (1842) dreams of annihilating all of creation by a huge conflagration, by setting fire to the great cities of the world. The dreams of Chateaubriand's René seem pallid indeed when compared with the hero's dreams in *Novembre* who sees himself galloping over populations and terrifying all men, as Nero once had terrified them, simply by a frown. There is exoticism in Chateaubriand, especially in passages of *Mémoires d'outre-tombe,* but there is little of Flaubert's lecherous cruel Orient. With Lautréamont, the style of such writing became more laconic, the description more bare, and the acts of violence more significant.

IX *Conclusion*

Romantic taste was traditionally for what is not known, not familiar, not directly experienced: Chateaubriand's America, Hugo's Spain, Musset's Italy, Flaubert's Carthage. Lautréamont moved beyond this easily identifiable Romantic exoticism. The settings of the action in *Les Chants de Maldoror* are recognizable in a fragmentary way, but they are for the most part abstract and give the impression of being a montage of landscapes and seascapes of a dream: the sea, the seashore, a field, a bordello, a mountain, a city park. Lautréamont is not the meticulous artist reconstructing a scene from historical documents as Flaubert did in *Salammbô* or Victor Hugo did in *Notre-Dame-de-Paris.* His landscapes are from the mind and from the memory of dreams and from the jumbled memory of books. Only a few words are necessary to paint the background against which we will see clearly, more clearly than the ordinary reader would like to see, a figure stalking another figure, a plot of murder unfolding, a picture of physical frustration, scenes, in a word, that we half remember from dreams and which we try to decipher in the light of day that usually dispels the power and the fascination of the dreams as they unfold in the freedom of the subconscious.

Whereas the dreams of history and exotic lands characterize the work of the Romantic artist, the literal dreams and the fantasy life of a young man characterize Lautréamont. Baudelaire was fully conscious when he characterized *les femmes damnées,* and Flaubert was fully conscious when he characterized Emma Bovary. There are no such characterizations of Maldoror or of the various person- ages he encounters throughout *Les Chants.* Cruelty and baseness are described and analyzed by the Romantics, by Baudelaire and Flaubert, and such themes are always attached to man's unhappi- ness. They are antagonistic to the experience of happiness which is not a subject for the Romantic artist.

This cleavage, this separation in man's nature and man's behavior, this duality of good and evil, of happiness and unhappi- ness, of heaven and hell, of chastity and orgy, this endless antinomy between apparent opposites: day and night, white and black, het- erosexual and homosexual, conscious and subconscious—is the very basis of Western civilization as we know it. It is the basis of customs and laws that have governed man since the birth of Chris- tianity.

The so-called movement of decadence, with the central figure of Lautréamont, not recognized as such in the historical age of deca- dence, but seen more clearly to be that central figure from our perspective today, questioned that dichotomy of good and evil, of female and male, of life and death, of love and hate, of young and old. He questioned it, as he leaned heavily on the indications behind him proposed by Sade and Baudelaire in particular, and opened up the way to the Surrealists who followed him and who proclaimed the fusion of the opposites, the joining of the two domains of the conscious and the subconscious, of the equal reality of day and night, of the sun-flooded life of man and the oneiric scenes that fill his nights.

Selected Bibliography

1. Bibliographies (All three are excellent and almost complete.)

WALZER, PIERRE OLIVIER, *Oeuvres complètes de Lautréamont et Germain Nouveau*. Bibliothèque de la Pléiade, Gallimard, 1970.

Entretiens, No. 30. "Lautréamont," bibliographie établie par Rosy Chaleil. 1971.

PHILIP, MICHEL, *Lectures de Lautréamont*. Colin, 1971.

2. Biographies (both correct misinterpretations and provide information on family, acquaintances, and places where Ducasse lived).

CARADEC, FRANÇOIS, *Isidore Ducasse, comte de Lautréamont*. La Table Ronde, 1970.

PEYROUZET, E., *Vie de Lautréamont*. Grasset, 1970.

PRIMARY SOURCES

Editions

Les Chants de Maldoror (Bruxelles: Imprimerie de A. Lacroix, Verboeckhoven et Cie, 1869). The first edition. Not put on sale.

Poésies I, II. Isidore Ducasse (Paris: Librairie Gabrie, 1870).

Les Chants de Maldoror. Bruxelles, 1874. This is the edition of 1869. Only the cover was changed.

Les Chants de Maldoror (Paris: L. Genonceaux, 1890). Preface by Genonceaux.

Poésies I. Published in Littérature, No. 2. April, 1919, with note by A. Breton. *Poésies II. ibid.* May, 1919.

Les Chants de Maldoror (Paris: La Sirène, 1920). Préface de Gourmont.

Oeuvres complètes. Etude, commentaire et notes par Philippe Soupault (Paris: Au Sans-Pareil, 1927).

SECONDARY SOURCES

1. Articles and Chapters on Lautréamont

BALAKIAN, ANNA. *Surrealism: the Road to the Absolute* (New York: E. P. Dutton, 1970). Chapter 2, "Lautréamont's Battle with God," is a succinct statement on the imagery and the themes of Lautréamont that attracted the Surrealists.

BERNARD, SUZANNE. *Le poème en prose de Baudelaire à nos jours.* Nizet, 1959. Chapter 3 of the first part of this book, is a study of "Lautréamont et la Poésie frénétique," in which the critic analyzes the genre of *Les Chants de Maldoror.* Is the work a novel or a series of prose poems?

BONNET, MARGUERITE. "Lautréamont et Michelet" *Revue d'histoire littéraire de la France.* Oct.–déc., 1964. A very precise and useful study of Lautréamont's use of Michelet.

CAMUS, ALBERT. *L'homme révolté.* Gallimard, 1951. (see Chapter 5 in this book.)

CÉSAIRE, AIMÉ. *"Isidore Ducasse, comte de Lautréamont,"* Tropiques, fév., 1943 (see Chapter 5).

FOWLIE, WALLACE. *Age of Surrealism.* Indiana Univ. Press, 1960. Chapter 2 in this book is a study of Lautréamont's temperament and its relationship to Surrealism.

————, *Love in Literature.* Indiana Univ. Press, 1965. The chapter on Lautréamont is an analysis of the passage in *Les Chants* where God and Maldoror are called "two neighboring monarchs," one fearing the other.

————, *Climate of Violence.* Macmillan, 1967. Under the general theme of "Violence," Lautréamont's epic is studied in its relation to the violence in Baudelaire's poems on Paris and Rimbaud's *Saison en enfer.*

GIDE, ANDRÉ. *Journal, 1889–1939.* Gallimard, 1939. In the entry of Nov. 28, 1905, Gide, in just a few sentences records his impression of the sixth canto of *Les Chants.*

GREENE, THOMAS. "The Relevance of Lautréamont," *Partisan Review.* Sept., 1954. A brilliant analysis of the continuing significance of Lautréamont today.

MILLER, HENRY. "Let us be content with three little new-born elephants," *Accent,* Autumn, 1944 (see Chapter 5).

SOLLERS, PHILIPPE. *Logiques.* Seuil, 1968 (see Chapter 5).

2. Special Issues of Periodicals

Le cas Lautréamont. Le Disque vert. Paris-Bruxelles, 1925.
Lautréamont n'a pas cent ans. Cahiers du Sud. août, 1946.
Lautréamont. L'Arc, 1967.
Lautréamont. Entretiens, 1971.

Index